I0540455

MARK BIBLE STUDY

DISCOVER THE TRANSFORMATIVE TRUTHS OF JESUS

40-DAY BIBLE STUDY SERIES
BOOK 14

PETER DEHAAN

Mark Bible Study: Discover the Transformative Truths of Jesus

Copyright © 2025 by Peter DeHaan.

40-Day Bible Study Series, Book 14

All rights reserved: No part of this book may be reproduced, disseminated, or transmitted in any form, by any means, or for any purpose, without the express written consent of the author or his legal representatives. The only exceptions are brief excerpts, and the cover image, for reviews or academic research. For permissions: peterdehaan.com/contact.

All Scripture quotations, unless otherwise indicated, are taken from the Holy Bible, New International Version®, NIV®. Copyright © 1973, 1978, 1984, 2011 by Biblica, Inc. ™ Used by permission of Zondervan. All rights reserved worldwide. www.zondervan.com The "NIV" and "New International Version" are trademarks registered in the United States Patent and Trademark Office by Biblica, Inc.™

Library of Congress Control Number: 2025905951

Published by Rock Rooster Books, Grand Rapids, Michigan

ISBN:

- 979-8-88809-138-8 (ebook)
- 979-8-88809-139-5 (paperback)
- 979-8-88809-140-1 (hardcover)
- 979-8-88809-141-8 (audiobook)

Credits:

- Developmental editor: Julie Harbison
- Copyeditor: Robyn Mulder
- Cover design: Fanderclai Design
- Author photo: Chelsie Jensen Photography

To Bonnie DeHaan

Series by Peter DeHaan

40-Day Bible Study Series takes a fresh and practical look into Scripture, book by book.

Bible Character Sketches Series celebrates people in Scripture, from the well-known to the obscure.

Holiday Celebration Devotionals rejoice in the holidays with Jesus.

Visiting Churches Series takes an in-person look at church practices and traditions to inform and inspire today's followers of Jesus.

Be the first to hear about Peter's new books and receive updates at PeterDeHaan.com/updates.

CONTENTS

Mark and His Book about Jesus   1

Day 1: John the Baptist   4

Day 2: Jesus Prepares for Ministry   7

Day 3: Jesus Heals   11

Day 4: Jesus Seeks Solitude   14

Day 5: Jesus Saves and Heals   18

Day 6: Fasting   21

Bonus Content: Only Sick People
Need a Doctor   24

Day 7: Sabbath   26

Day 8: Blasphemy   29

Day 9: The Parable of the Sower   32

Bonus Content: Never Understanding   35

Day 10: More Lessons   38

Day 11: Jesus Controls the Weather   41

Day 12: Demons and Pigs   44

Day 13: Healing and Resurrection   47

Day 14: The First Missionaries   50

Day 15: John the Baptist   53

Day 16: Supernatural Power   56

Day 17: Jesus Clarifies the Law   59

Day 18: Two More Healings   63

Day 19: Bread and Yeast   67

Day 20: Don't Tell Anyone   70

Day 21: Get Behind Me Satan   74

Day 22: I Believe!   77

Bonus Content: The Transfiguration   80

Day 23: Welcome the Children   83

Day 24: Leave It All Behind   86
Day 25: Be a Servant   90
Day 26: A House of Prayer   93
Day 27: Move Mountains   97
Day 28: The Top Two   100
Day 29: God's Perspective on Giving   104
Day 30: Watch Out   107
Day 31: The End Is Near   110
Day 32: The Lord's Supper   113
Bonus Content: Jesus Anointed   116
Day 33: Jesus's Prayer   118
Day 34: Deserting Jesus   121
Bonus Content: Mark References the
Old Testament   124
Day 35: I Am   127
Day 36: Peter Falters   130
Day 37: Jesus Mocked and Killed   134
Day 38: An Unexpected Testimony   138
Day 39: Jesus Resurrects   142
Day 40: Last Instructions   146

Books in the 40-Day Bible Study Series   150
For Small Groups, Sunday School, and
Classes   152
If You're New to the Bible   154
About Peter DeHaan   157
Books by Peter DeHaan   159

MARK AND HIS BOOK ABOUT JESUS

The book of Mark, named after its author, is one of the four Gospels in the Bible. Each one is a biography that focuses on the life, ministry, death, and resurrection of Jesus.

Mark's book is the shortest and most concise of the four Gospels. It's an ideal source to gain a quick and essential understanding of who Jesus is and what he did. Though Mark may not include some of the delightful details we read in the other Gospels, he provides us with the critical elements of Jesus's life and ministry. As such, the book of Mark is a great place to start.

The books of Matthew and Luke have many parallel passages to what we read in Mark, but this is not the case with the book of John.

The Gospel of Mark, likely written by John Mark, is considered the first Gospel written. It's a fast-moving narrative, clearly communicated in dramatic description. It is simultaneously simple yet also equally profound.

We first read about John Mark in Acts. His mother's name is Mary. Jesus's followers are having a prayer meeting at her house, asking God to release Peter from prison. John Mark doesn't play any role in the story, but the author of Acts feels it's important that we know he's present.

John Mark is a cousin of Barnabas. Barnabas wants to take John Mark with him and Paul (also called Saul) on one of their mission trips. Paul objects because John Mark had deserted them on a previous journey, but Barnabas sees potential in his younger cousin.

Paul and Barnabas debate the issue, but they can't reach a consensus. Their pointed dispute over John Mark causes them to end their partnership and stop working together. Though a sad development, this allows them to cover more territory and mentor other people. God turns their disagreement into something good.

Based on this event, we may assume Paul has no

use for John Mark and writes him off. But this isn't true.

The two of them reconcile. We get a hint of this at the end of Paul's second letter to Timothy. There Paul instructs his protégé: "When you come, bring John Mark with you, for he's helpful to me in my work." Furthermore, Paul notes that John Mark is with him when he writes to his friend Philemon.

Though John Mark initially proves himself unworthy, he turns things around and wins Paul's approval. Though John Mark didn't start out well, he finished strong.

When we flounder, do we give up or push through to turn things around? Who must we reconcile with? Who can we mentor?

[Discover more about John Mark in Acts 12:12, Acts 12:25, Acts 13:13, Acts 15:36–41, Colossians 4:10, 2 Timothy 4:11, Philemon 1:23–24, and 1 Peter 5:13. Though not all these passages specify John Mark, the context suggests they all cover the same person.]

DAY 1: JOHN THE BAPTIST
MARK 1:1–8

And this was his message: "After me comes the one more powerful than I, the straps of whose sandals I am not worthy to stoop down and untie." (Mark 1:7)

Unlike the openings to the other three gospel accounts of Jesus's life, Mark skips the buildup and goes directly to the story. There's no genealogy (as with Matthew), nativity story (Luke), or poetic prologue (John). Mark just gives the essential facts.

In this way, Mark's account opens with John the Baptist. But it's not John the Baptist's birth. Instead, it's his ministry—some thirty years later. John's ministry serves as the prelude to Jesus's, which we'll get to in Day 2.

Mark begins his story with Isaiah's prophecy. But this isn't a prophecy of Jesus. Instead, it foresees the one who will precede Jesus: John the Baptist.

Quoting the Old Testament text, Mark writes that God will send his messenger ahead of the Messiah. The messenger will serve as the advance team for the expected Savior. The messenger will tell people to prepare for the Lord, to make the paths straight for him.

This prophecy comes from Isaiah 40:3, as well as Malachi 3:1.

The people are to repent of their sins and be baptized. This prepares them to accept Jesus and follow him.

Baptism is a New Testament concept; the word does not appear in the Old Testament. Though some Bible scholars connect baptism with the ceremonial washings prescribed in the Old Testament, Peter has a better explanation. He connects baptism with the flood when God saves Noah and his family from judgment (1 Peter 3:19–22). In essence, Noah and his family were symbolically baptized. God saved them.

Paul gives another Old Testament connection to

baptism through Moses (1 Corinthians 10:2). Their baptism comes through the cloud that guided the people in the wilderness and when the sea parted to let them escape Egypt.

John the Baptist says he isn't even worthy to untie Jesus's sandals. This is an appropriately humble attitude, one we should all model in our relationship with our Lord. Yet Jesus later says John is the greatest of all men. But when we follow Jesus, we will all become greater than John the Baptist (Matthew 11:11 and Luke 7:28).

John will baptize the people with water, but Jesus will baptize people with the Holy Spirit. This is certainly exciting news for us to look forward to as we read the book of Mark—as well as for our own lives.

What do we think about the ministry of John the Baptist? How can we show that we have repented from our sins?

[Discover another prophecy about John the Baptist, symbolically represented by Elijah, in Malachi 4:5–6.]

DAY 2: JESUS PREPARES FOR MINISTRY

MARK 1:9–20

And a voice came from heaven: "You are my Son, whom I love; with you I am well pleased." (Mark 1:11)

I n Day 1, we established that John the Baptist came to prepare the way for the expected and promised Messiah, Jesus. John does this by baptizing people for the repentance of their sins.

With this as the background, we now see Jesus for the first time in Mark's book. Jesus comes to John and asks the baptizer to baptize him.

Does this seem odd? It should.

John's baptism is for people who repent from their sins. They admit the wrong things they've done in their life. They wish to turn their life around and go in a new direction. John baptizes them so they can publicly show their decision.

This doesn't apply to Jesus. He's sinless. He doesn't need to repent of anything or be baptized. Yet he asks John the Baptizer to do just that.

As Jesus comes out of the water after his baptism, heaven opens and the Holy Spirit descends from heaven like a dove, resting on him. This shows the Holy Spirit infilling Jesus and being part of him.

A voice booms from heaven. "You are my Son. I love you so much. You please me." This is the voice of Father God proclaiming Jesus as his Son. This affirms Jesus for his character.

The Holy Spirit sends Jesus into the wilderness —the desert. Jesus stays there for forty days. During this time, Satan tempts him.

Mark doesn't share about Jesus fasting, being hungry, or the enemy's assaults in the desert. He merely says that Satan tempts Jesus. Knowing Jesus's character, Mark doesn't need to tell us that Jesus prevails. We know he does.

These actions prepare Jesus for ministry. The Father affirms him, and the Spirit fills him. Jesus also prevails over Satan. Now he is ready to begin his work.

Mark includes an interesting detail that Jesus doesn't begin proclaiming the good news until after John lands in prison. Their ministries are consecutive, not overlapping. John's ministry ends, and Jesus's ministry begins. John the Baptist confirms this transition, as written by John the apostle (John 3:30).

Not only does Jesus begin with a call for the people to repent and believe, he also invites others to follow him. As he walks along the shore of the lake, he comes across two brothers fishing. They are Simon (later called Peter) and Andrew. Jesus says, "Come, follow me, and I will send you out to fish for people."

What a powerful way for Jesus to cast a vision. He takes the routine of what they're doing, fishing to earn money, and turns it into a metaphor for a mission. Instead of seeking fish to sell to survive, Jesus calls these two men into something greater, to seek people for his kingdom. He then invites two more fishermen to join them: James and John.

This marks another preparation for ministry— for both Jesus and for us: people to work with. We are not to proceed alone (Ecclesiastes 4:9–12). We'll expand on this a bit in Day 14.

The Father affirms Jesus. The Holy Spirit fills

Jesus. The tempter is dismissed by Jesus. And people agree to go with Jesus.

How are we doing at following Jesus? How can we apply Jesus's preparation for ministry to our own faith journey?

[Discover more about baptism in Acts 13:24–25, Acts 18:24–26, and Acts 19:1–6.]

DAY 3: JESUS HEALS

MARK 1:21–34

Jesus healed many who had various diseases. He also drove out many demons. (Mark 1:34)

After preparing himself for ministry and calling his first four disciples, Jesus goes to the synagogue to teach. His style differs from what the people usually hear. He doesn't repeat what other teachers have said. Instead, he gives them fresh instruction. He speaks with authority. This sharply contrasts with how the teachers of the law communicate.

In the middle of Jesus's message, a man possessed by an impure spirit interrupts the

Teacher. He challenges Jesus, questions Jesus, and declares who Jesus is.

Jesus tells the impure spirit to be quiet and leave the man. With a violent shake and a loud shriek, the demon does exactly what Jesus commanded him to do. This amazes the people.

Jesus teaches with authority, and evil spirits obey him. The news of what he did spreads quickly through the area.

Though we may question what an evil spirit is and how it relates to us today—or how it might not—the point is that this man's life was a mess, and Jesus made it better. That's what matters. Don't lose sight of this truth.

Jesus and his disciples leave the synagogue and go to Simon and Andrew's home. Simon's mother-in-law has an incapacitating fever. Jesus takes her by the hand and helps her stand. The fever leaves her, and she is fine.

Based on the news of Jesus's miraculous work, people of the area bring the sick and demon-possessed to him. With the whole town gathered to witness it, Jesus heals their diseases and drives out demons.

Jesus came to earth to both heal and to save. Two thousand years ago, the people flocked to Jesus for his healing power, but most missed his saving power.

Today it's the opposite for most people. We come to Jesus to save us, but we don't rely on him to heal us. Instead, we turn to modern medicine when we have a health issue. We typically involve Jesus as an afterthought, if we involve him at all. Perhaps we should take the opposite approach.

Not only does Jesus save us, but he also heals us —if only we will come to him. But we must first come to him if we are to receive what he offers.

How well do we do at trusting Jesus to save us? How well do we do at trusting Jesus to heal us?

[Discover more about Jesus's healing power in Mark 6:13 and his saving power in Mark 16:16.]

DAY 4: JESUS SEEKS SOLITUDE
MARK 1:35–45

Very early in the morning, while it was still dark, Jesus got up, left the house and went off to a solitary place, where he prayed. (Mark 1:35)

The next story Mark shares is about Jesus getting up early in the morning to pray. We don't know if this occurs the day after he heals all the people of their diseases and casts out impure spirits or if this occurs some days later. Or, since this was a regular practice of Jesus, Mark may simply include the account at this point in his narrative.

There are three key elements of what Jesus does. First, it's early in the morning. Second, he wants to be alone. Third, he prays. Let's explore these three elements.

First, consider what time it is. It's early in the morning, while it's still dark. We may conclude that we should seek God in the morning before we begin our day.

Though this is wise advice, let's be cautious about turning it into a rule. Some people may find it better to spend time with God at the end of their day, or even in the middle of it. When we spend time with God is not nearly so important as the fact that we do it. We should make spending time with God a regular habit.

Also note that it was still dark. This means it wasn't convenient. Not only did Jesus cut his sleep short to spend time with Papa, but he also had to walk in the dark.

Next, Jesus leaves the house and goes to a solitary place. He doesn't want others to distract him from focusing on the Father. Though we can certainly connect with God when other people are around, it will be better and deeper if we seek solitude first. This allows us to focus our attention on the Almighty without the distractions of people or life to get in our way.

Last, we read that Jesus prayed. This stands as

his purpose for getting up early and seeking solitude. He wants to connect with his Father in Heaven.

Though we don't know what Jesus prayed, or the nature of his interaction, it may be best to consider it more as a dialogue than a monologue. When prayer is a dialogue with God, we speak and we listen. Better yet is when we listen first and then speak later—if we even need to speak at all.

Yet many of our prayers today—if not all of them—are monologues. We give God our list of requests and take no time to first gain his assessment of the situation. I suspect that if we listened first and then prayed, there'd be many prayers we wouldn't even need to make. We'd realize they were selfish and misaligned with God's perspective.

May Jesus's example inform how we pray and how we spend time with God.

Is our prayer time with God more like a dialogue or a monologue? How often do we get up early and seek solitude to spend time with God?

[Discover another time when Jesus sought solitude in Mark 6:32.]

DAY 5: JESUS SAVES AND HEALS
MARK 2:1–12

"Which is easier: to say to this paralyzed man, 'Your sins are forgiven,' or to say, 'Get up, take your mat and walk'?"
(Mark 2:9)

I n Day 3 we discussed that Jesus came to heal and to save. Both aspects of this dual role of his ministry brilliantly emerge in this powerful story of Jesus and the paralyzed man.

After Jesus heals a man of his leprosy, the people come to him from everywhere. He tries to avoid attracting attention to himself (Mark 1:43–45).

A few days later, Jesus teaches inside a house. The place is packed. Some men bring a paralyzed friend to him, but they can't get inside to reach Jesus. In desperation, they climb onto the roof, make an opening in it, and lower their friend before Jesus.

I wonder why they didn't just wait outside for Jesus to leave and ask him to heal their friend then. It seems like the simpler solution. Yet perhaps they're so focused on getting the help their friend desperately needs that they're not willing to wait. They see an opportunity, and they seize it. I also wonder if they damaged the roof and what the homeowner might have thought about it.

Nevertheless, Jesus finds his teaching interrupted when this paralyzed man descends from the ceiling, suspended in front of him.

Jesus stops his message, for another teachable moment has presented itself.

It's obvious the man is paralyzed, and his pressing need is to walk. Many of the people there likely know this man and his situation.

Mark writes that Jesus sees their faith—the faith of the man's friends. In a surprise move, Jesus confounds everybody by forgiving the man's sins.

Jesus knows this man's greatest need isn't physical but spiritual, so he addresses it first. By offering the man forgiveness, Jesus saves him from his sins. Saving people is one reason Jesus came to earth.

The religious leaders criticize Jesus in their minds. He knows their thoughts and confronts them. He asks them a simple question. "Is it easier to say, 'I forgive your sins' or 'Get up and walk'?"

Anyone can forgive another, but few have God's healing power to restore a paralyzed man.

Knowing it's much easier to say "I forgive your sins" than to make a lame man walk, Jesus heals the man. This addresses the man's second greatest need. In doing so, Jesus proves he also has the power to forgive sins.

In this account, Jesus shows he came not only to save (forgive our sins) but also to heal.

Jesus saves, and Jesus heals.

What do we look to Jesus to do for us? When someone comes to us for help, do we address their biggest need first?

[Discover more about the forgiveness of sins in Psalm 32:1–2, Ephesians 1:7–10, and Colossians 1:13–14.]

DAY 6: FASTING
MARK 2:13–22

Jesus answered, "How can the guests of the bridegroom fast while he is with them? They cannot, so long as they have him with them." (Mark 2:19)

Though we may think the Old Testament of the Bible commands us to fast as a regular practice, it doesn't appear to do so. The closest passage is the instruction about the Day of Atonement, when the people are told to deny themselves (Leviticus 23:27–28). This implies fasting.

We do, however, see specific commands to fast in the writings of the prophets as they proclaim God's instructions (Isaiah 58:6 and Joel 2:12). The first is to expand the meaning of a fast beyond an abstinence from food; the second is a call to repent. David also fasts as a sign of repentance (Psalm 35:13 and Psalm 69:10).

Next, we see the example of Ezra declaring a fast (Ezra 8:21), as well as Esther (Esther 4:16). Both fasts are to seek God's favor for the challenges that loom before them.

Though all these Old Testament references to fasting address specific instances, fasting emerges as a regular practice by the time we get to the New Testament.

Jesus began his ministry by fasting for forty days (Matthew 4:1–2). He later taught about the right way to fast (Matthew 6:16–18). He even shared a story of a man who boasted about fasting twice a week (Luke 18:10–12).

Before Jesus's birth, Anna spent her time in the temple worshiping, fasting, and praying (Luke 2:36–37). And after Jesus returned to heaven, the early church also fasted (Acts 13:1–3 and Acts 14:23).

Yet aside from Jesus's initial fast before he began his ministry, there's no other mention of him fasting. There's also no mention of Jesus's disciples ever fasting when he was with them.

The people confront Jesus on his apparent

double standard. "John's disciples fasted, and the Pharisees' disciples fast. Why don't yours?" they ask.

Jesus tells them that there's no need for his disciples to fast because he's with them. It's a time of celebration. Yet when he leaves, their time to fast will return.

When we view fasting as a means to approach God and connect with him on a deeper, more intimate level, there's no need for the disciples to fast. Jesus is in their very presence. That's as good as it gets. They should celebrate that reality. There's no need to fast to achieve what they already have.

Yet when Jesus leaves, the time to fast will return. Jesus says so. This is so they may better connect with God.

How should we view fasting? How important is it for us to practice fasting?

[Discover more about fasting in 2 Samuel 12:15–18, Nehemiah 9:1, Jeremiah 36:9, Daniel 9:3, and Zechariah 7:1–7.]

BONUS CONTENT: ONLY SICK PEOPLE NEED A DOCTOR

On hearing this, Jesus said to them, "It is not the healthy who need a doctor, but the sick. I have not come to call the righteous, but sinners." (Mark 2:17)

After Jesus calls Levi to follow him, he goes to Levi's house for dinner. Joining them at the meal are many people the religious leaders look down on: tax collectors and sinners. The religious leaders criticize Jesus for spending time with these folks.

Jesus tells them healthy people don't need a doctor, but the sick do. He didn't come for those who are righteous, but for sinners.

Since he came to heal and to save, we can

comprehend this both literally and figuratively, that is, the physically sick and the spiritually sick.

Jesus came for sinners, for those who miss the mark. Conversely, Jesus did not come for the healthy, the righteous. What exactly does this mean?

It could mean that since the religious leaders consider themselves healthy, there's nothing Jesus can do for them. Although they really are sick, he can't be their doctor until they admit they are ill.

Jesus came for those who are sick. He came for you and for me.

Spiritually, we all need a doctor, but are we willing to admit it? Do we rely on our righteousness to save us or on Jesus?

[Discover more about righteousness in Matthew 5:20.]

DAY 7: SABBATH
MARK 2:23–3:12

Then he said to them, "The Sabbath was made for man, not man for the Sabbath." (Mark 2:27)

We often see Jesus healing people on the Sabbath, much to the religious leaders' dismay. They embraced the seventh day as a day of rest when they should do no work (Exodus 23:12).

When God gives his people this instruction, they had just been freed from slavery. As slaves, they worked every day and never got a day off. They had no weekend. They enjoyed no rest. Their masters saw to that.

When they became free, God gives them a day

off. It's a day to rest when they don't have to work. What a relief. To guide them in this day off, he shifts their attention from endless labor to him. They're to make the day holy and do no work (Exodus 31:14–16).

In this, we see a principle of the seventh day being given to us for our benefit and not something to restrict us. It was made for us, not the other way around.

Does this mean we're free to do whatever we want on Sunday? Maybe. Maybe not. Does this mean we can treat Sunday like every other day? Maybe. Maybe not.

One Sabbath, Jesus and his disciples walk through a grain field. The disciples pick some heads of grain as they pass by.

In the legalistic minds of the Pharisees, this is harvesting grain and constitutes labor, which goes against God's command to not work on the seventh day. The Pharisees criticize the disciples for breaking the law.

Jesus counters with an example of when King David broke the law without reproof.

Then Jesus says, "The Sabbath was made for man, not man for the Sabbath." In this he confirms we aren't beholden to this special day, held captive by it, or restricted in any way. Instead, it's a day for us to enjoy.

This means we must shove aside legalistic ideas of what we may and may not do. Instead, we must embrace our seventh day for the freedom it gives us. How we do so is for us to determine.

On another Sabbath, Jesus goes to the synagogue. A man with a deformed hand is there. The Pharisees watch Jesus closely to see what he will do.

Jesus has the man stand. He asks the crowd if the Sabbath is a time to do good or evil, to save life or to kill. It's a rhetorical question.

Then Jesus heals the man. In this way, he shows us that the Sabbath is a time to do good and help make people's lives better.

Is it correct to apply teachings about the Sabbath in the Bible to our Sunday today? What can we use to guide us in our Sunday practices?

[Discover more about how to treat our days in Romans 14:5. Also consider Ecclesiastes 3:1–8.]

DAY 8: BLASPHEMY

MARK 3:13–34

"Whoever blasphemes against the Holy Spirit will never be forgiven; they are guilty of an eternal sin." (Mark 3:29)

J esus has already called five of his disciples. First were the four fishermen: Simon, Andrew, James, and John. Fifth was Levi (Matthew), the tax collector.

Now Jesus adds seven more to round out his list to twelve. They are Philip, Bartholomew, Thomas, James (Alphaeus's son), Thaddaeus, Simon the Zealot, and Judas Iscariot. Jesus wants to train them to send them out to preach the good news and have the authority to drive out demons. We'll cover this in Day 14.

After selecting the twelve, a large crowd gathers. There are so many people—expecting so much—that Jesus and his disciples don't even have time to eat. Thinking he's losing his mind, his family heads there to intervene.

The religious leaders have a different perspective. They attribute Jesus's behavior to Beelzebub (Satan). They imply Jesus is demon-possessed. That's why he's able to drive out evil spirits.

Jesus counters their claim by pointing out their logic error. It would be like Satan trying to drive out Satan.

Then Jesus says people can receive forgiveness of all their sins, of every slander that they speak. This implies that Jesus views their accusation of him as sinful, as slander.

But he tacks on a chilling addendum. He says that whoever blasphemes the Holy Spirit will never be forgiven. It is an eternal sin.

This is a worrisome teaching, and we're left to wonder what it means. The context suggests that blasphemy against the Holy Spirit is denying his power or possibly attributing Holy Spirit power to the devil. May we avoid both errors.

By this time, Jesus's family arrives. They send

someone inside to call him, to let him know his mother and brothers are outside and want to talk.

Jesus doesn't leave.

Instead, he asks those gathered a seemingly rhetorical question, "Who are my mother and my brothers?"

Jesus scans the crowd to gaze at those sitting around him. I imagine him smiling as he gestures to them. "You are my mother and my brothers."

Just as we have a biological family of parents, siblings, and relatives, we also have a spiritual family of those who follow Jesus.

What is our attitude toward our biological family? How much do we value our spiritual family?

[Discover more about Jesus's biological family in Mark 6:3.]

DAY 9: THE PARABLE OF THE SOWER
MARK 4:1–20

Then Jesus said to them, "Don't you understand this parable? How then will you understand any parable?" (Mark 4:13)

J esus teaches the people. They're at a lake. The crowd pushes toward him. He gets in a boat and pushes away from the shore. Not only does this give him a buffer between himself and the people, it also helps them hear him because sound travels better over water than land.

He gives them a parable, which is how he normally speaks to the masses. It's the parable of the sower.

He invites the people to envision a farmer going out to his field to plant seed. In that day, farmers seeded their land by broadcasting it with their hand. It was slow and inefficient. Yet it was their only means to plant.

Despite the farmer's careful sowing, some of the seed falls on the path. Birds swoop in and eat it.

Other seed falls among rocks, but there isn't much dirt. It springs up quickly but has little roots. It soon dies.

A third batch of seed falls among the thorns. As the seed grows, so do the thorns. The thorns choke out the plants, and it doesn't yield a crop.

The last group of seed falls on good soil. It sprouts, grows, and produces a harvest. It yields a thirty, sixty, and even one-hundred-fold return. This seed is most productive.

Later, Jesus's disciples and followers ask him why he speaks in parables. They're likely confused by his message. Then Jesus explains the meaning of the parable of the sower to them.

The seed the farmer sows is the word given to all people, as represented by the different types of ground.

The seed that falls on the path and is snatched away by birds is like people who hear God's good news, but Satan comes along and steals it.

The people represented by the rocky terrain

hear God's news and receive it with much joy. It sprouts, but since it never takes root in their lives, it doesn't withstand life's troubles or worldly persecutions.

For the seed planted among thorns, life's worries, the distraction of money, and human desires choke its message. Though it lives, it produces no fruit.

Yet the seed among the good soil is God's word shared to people with open hearts. They hear it, accept it, and produce a crop.

This is why the farmer planted the field. This is the outcome he wanted.

May we likewise produce a bountiful harvest for Jesus.

What part of this parable do we find most surprising? Which of this parable's illustrations best represents us?

[Discover more about sowing the good news of Jesus in 1 Corinthians 3:6–8.]

BONUS CONTENT: NEVER UNDERSTANDING

[Jesus] told them, "The secret of the kingdom of God has been given to you. But to those on the outside everything is said in parables." (Mark 4:11)

In the middle of the passage we read for Day 9, Mark inserts another teaching into the lesson about the sower. It falls between Jesus sharing the parable with everyone and explaining its meaning to his followers.

In defending why he uses parables, he quotes from the prophet Isaiah. With parables, some will see but not perceive; they will hear but not understand. Otherwise, they might turn to God and receive his forgiveness (Isaiah 6:9–10).

On the surface, it seems that Jesus intentionally hides his good news from all but a select few.

Yet this understanding contradicts a clearer passage in Scripture. Peter writes that the Lord does not want anyone to perish but to come to him in repentance (2 Peter 3:9). Note that this isn't a promise that all will be saved, merely that our Lord wishes this for everyone. Since we have free will, the choice ultimately falls to each person.

Instead, we're better off to understand this perplexing passage in Mark as saying that those who follow Jesus will understand, while those who have rejected him will not. This may be a repeated, ultimate rejection of Jesus's saving work. Those who say no to Jesus have closed their mind and their heart to him; they therefore cannot understand what he offers.

Paul confirms this. He writes that Jesus's good news is nothing more than foolishness to those who are perishing (1 Corinthians 1:18–25).

Yet if there are some elements of Jesus's teaching that we don't quite comprehend, we should not despair. The disciples struggled too. That's why Jesus explained the parable to them. If the disciples needed help, we shouldn't worry if we also need a bit of help.

Not only do we have Jesus's words in the Bible to guide us, we also have the Holy Spirit to help us understand what it says (John 14:26).

What do we do when we encounter a confusing passage in the Bible? How often do we turn to the Holy Spirit for clarity?

[Discover more about sowing seed in Proverbs 11:18, 2 Corinthians 9:10, and Galatians 6:7–8.]

DAY 10: MORE LESSONS
MARK 4:21–34

With many similar parables Jesus spoke the word to them, as much as they could understand. (Mark 4:33)

After sharing with us Jesus's parable of the sower, along with his explanation, Mark adds several more teachings. We don't know if Jesus explains the meaning of these parables or not, but if he does, Mark doesn't share them. Yet by knowing Jesus's explanation of the parable of the sower, we have insight into how to interpret his other teachings and parables.

First, we have the parable of a lamp on a stand. We use a lamp to illuminate the space around us so we can see, to give us light. To maximize its utility, we place the light on a stand.

Metaphorically, we need to let our light shine for Jesus. We don't want to hide his good news from others. We need to bring it out into the open. Then we'll produce a good yield, just like the seed that fell on the good soil in the parable of the sower (Day 9).

A parallel teaching emerges from this image. Jesus says that whatever is hidden will be disclosed; what is concealed will be brought into the open. This gives us two considerations.

One is that the shameful things we do in secret will not stay hidden. Others will one day see them. How humiliating for us. Yet we should be even more embarrassed that God already knows what we did.

The counter-perspective is that the good things we do for others in secret will also come to light. Others will one day know what we did and celebrate our deeds.

This thought flows into a third teaching. It's about generosity and stinginess. The measurement we use for others will be the measurement we receive.

Following this is that whoever has will receive more, and whoever has little will lose what he has.

This may be an ultra-concise summary of the parable of the bags of gold (Matthew 25:14–30) and the parable of the ten minas (Luke 19:11–26).

Next is a parable of the growing seed. We may expect it to be a repeat of the parable of the sower, but it isn't. A farmer plants seed in his field. What he does after that doesn't matter. It sprouts and grows on its own. It produces a crop. Then he harvests it. Yet between the planting and the harvesting, the farmer does little to make it grow—except to pray. He trusts God for the results. This is what the kingdom of God is like.

Last is the parable of the mustard seed. What starts as a small seed grows to become the largest plant in the garden. So too with the kingdom of God. It starts as a tiny seed and grows into something quite remarkable.

Which of these parables give us the most encouragement? Which of these parables challenge us to live our lives differently?

[Discover more about a mustard seed in Matthew 17:20.]

DAY 11: JESUS CONTROLS THE WEATHER
MARK 4:35–41

He said to his disciples, "Why are you so afraid? Do you still have no faith?" (Mark 4:40)

We've already seen Jesus heal the sick and cast out demons. And we'll soon see him raise the dead. These miracles that show his supernatural power all relate to people. Yet Jesus's power isn't limited to people. He is the master of all creation, including the weather.

After Jesus concludes his marathon teaching session of parables, he tells his disciples that he wants to go to the other side of the lake. Remember that Jesus is already sitting in a boat, which he used as a platform for his teaching.

Leaving the crowd behind, the disciples hoist their anchor and set out across the lake. There are other boats with them too. We don't know if some of his twelve disciples are in these boats or if it's some of his other followers, but there's more than one boat.

As they head out, Jesus wants to rest. He's likely exhausted after teaching the people all day. He goes to the back of the boat, finds a comfortable place, and lies down. Jesus falls asleep.

Yet Jesus may not get as much rest as he wants.

A storm brews. It turns into a furious squall. The waters rage, with huge waves breaking over the side of the boat. It nearly sinks them.

Though some of Jesus's disciples are experienced fishermen and know what it's like to encounter a storm on open water, this unnerves them. Fearing for their lives, they awake the sleeping Savior. "Teacher, doesn't it bother you that we're about to drown?"

I imagine Jesus being a little irked at having his needed rest interrupted.

Jesus gets up from his nap. He rebukes the wind, telling it to stop. "Quiet!" Then he chastises the waves. "Be still!"

The wind dies down and the waves dissipate,

leaving the water completely calm. Jesus has saved them from the peril. His power amazes them.

I now imagine Jesus shaking his head at his disciples. "Why were you so afraid? Have you no faith?"

As for their part, the disciples are terrified over what they just experienced, over what Jesus just did.

Once again, Jesus has surprised them.

What should our reaction be to Jesus controlling the weather? When confronted by life-threatening peril, how do we balance our fear with our faith?

[Discover more about the power Jesus gives us in John 14:12–14.]

DAY 12: DEMONS AND PIGS
MARK 5:1–20

Jesus did not let him [get in the boat], but said, "Go home to your own people and tell them how much the Lord has done for you, and how he has had mercy on you." (Mark 5:19)

J esus crosses the lake again. When he gets out of his boat, a man approaches. This is a man with an impure spirit. He comes from the tombs. This is where he lives.

The people have tried to restrain him, but ropes aren't strong enough—not even chains. He merely breaks them apart as if they are of no consequence. This may remind us of the powerful Samson breaking free of his restraints (Judges 16:12).

No one is strong enough to subdue this demon-possessed man. Perhaps this explains why he lives in the graveyard. People are less likely to bother him there. He spends his time wandering among the tombs and through the surrounding hills. He cries out and cuts himself with stones.

When the man sees Jesus, he runs to the Savior. He falls to his knees. But instead of repenting or seeking deliverance from his torment, the man shouts at Jesus. "What do you want with me? You're the Son of the Most High God. Don't torture me!" He says this in response to Jesus commanding the impure spirit to leave the man's body.

Jesus learns that the man is possessed by more than one spirit. These spirits go by the name of Legion, for many afflict this man. This is likely why he is in such torment.

Legion—speaking through the man—begs Jesus over and over to not send them away from the area. Instead, they request that Jesus send them into a nearby herd of pigs.

Jesus does.

The pigs go berserk, rush down the steep bank, and drown in the lake.

The people of the nearby town who hear what happened have two ways to respond:

In awe of Jesus's power and authority, they can

turn to him and follow him. Or, out of fear of the unknown and the uncomfortable, they can reject Jesus and push him away. They choose the latter, insisting that Jesus leave them alone and not bother them anymore. How sad.

How often are we confronted with the work of God, but—fearing the unknown or the uncomfortable—push him away?

The man is free of his tormenters. His sanity returns. He begs to go with Jesus, but the Teacher won't let him. Instead, Jesus instructs him to return home and tell his family and friends what God has done for him.

We should do the same.

How well have we done at telling our family and friends about Jesus? Do we stand in awe or tremble in fear when we see God's power?

[Discover more about impure spirits in Luke 11:24–26.]

DAY 13: HEALING AND
RESURRECTION

MARK 5:21–43

[Jesus] went in and said to them, "Why all this commotion and wailing? The child is not dead but asleep." (Mark 5:39)

After casting Legion out of the man, Jesus climbs back in the boat and leaves. When he reaches his destination, Jairus, the synagogue leader in that area, comes to Jesus and falls at his feet. He begs Jesus to heal his dying daughter.

Jesus agrees and goes with the man. A sizeable crowd follows.

Along the way, a woman who's suffered with bleeding for twelve years sees Jesus. She's desperate for a cure. She'd spent all her money on doctors, but they didn't help. They even made her situation worse. She believes if she can just place her hand on Jesus's cloak, she'll receive healing.

She pushes through the crowd, touches Jesus's garment, and her bleeding stops. She feels immediate relief.

Knowing that healing power flowed from his body, Jesus stops to ask who touched him. Given the crowd of people pressing around him, this seems like an unanswerable question.

Realizing what happened, the woman steps forward and admits it was her. Because of the woman's faith, Jesus proclaims healing and freedom for her.

But this delay costs Jairus. Word arrives from Jairus's house, telling him his daughter is dead. Jesus tells Jairus to not worry and just believe.

Jesus won't let the people follow him any further. He only takes Peter, James, and John with him as they continue to Jairus's house. When they reach Jairus's home, mourning for the girl has already begun.

"What's this all about?" Jesus asks. "She's not dead. She's merely sleeping."

Knowing the girl's dead, the people mock him. Jesus sends them away too.

Taking only the girl's parents and his three disciples, Jesus goes to the dead girl's body. He takes her by the hand and commands her to stand. She does. She walks around, and they give her something to eat.

For Jesus, raising someone from the dead is just as easy as it is for us to wake someone who's asleep.

First, Jesus heals the bleeding woman because of her faith. Then he resurrects the dead girl after telling her father to "just believe."

Is there nothing Jesus can't do?

Do we believe Jesus can heal us today? Would Jesus commend us for our faith or criticize it? (See Mark 4:40 and Mark 16:14.)

[Discover more about faith in Mark 2:5, Mark 10:52, and Mark 11:22–24.]

DAY 14: THE FIRST MISSIONARIES
MARK 6:1–13

They drove out many demons and anointed many sick people with oil and healed them. (Mark 6:13)

After Jesus raises the young girl from the dead, he goes home. When I think of home, I envision a safe place and a comfortable refuge. Yet this isn't what Jesus experiences.

The people he grew up with view him as a carpenter's son and nothing more. They take offense at his teaching and his miracles. The people's lack of faith limits what Jesus can do to help them.

He leaves his hometown and goes to other

villages to teach them. Then he sends out his twelve disciples in pairs, giving them authority over evil spirits.

Aside from John the Baptizer's preliminary work, they are the first missionaries for Jesus. They go out two by two. This is a wise decision.

King Solomon writes that two are better than one (Ecclesiastes 4:9–12). If one falls, the first can help the second get up; if they're by themselves, they struggle alone. Solomon concludes by saying a cord of three strands is strong. We need each other.

Another time Solomon writes that just as iron sharpens iron, one person sharpens another (Proverbs 27:17). Living by ourselves isn't good. The same applies to our faith. We need our brothers and sisters to help us become all we can be.

Jesus affirms Solomon's wisdom when he sends out his followers to spread his good news and help advance the kingdom. He sends them out two by two. Jesus knows that by sending them in pairs, they'll be more effective. They'll help each other, strengthening and encouraging them to complete their mission.

He tells them to take no provisions with them, implying they're to rely on God to provide for their needs. But he'll later tell them to do the opposite and to plan before they leave (Luke 22:35–37).

Jesus also tells them when they find a place to stay, to remain there until they leave town. If the town won't listen to them, they're to leave that place, shaking the dust off their feet as they depart. This suggests they're responsible for sharing the good news but not for the outcome.

They do as he says, spreading through the region to tell people about Jesus and encourage them to repent of their sins. As they do, they drive out demons and heal the sick.

When serving God, should we rely on him to provide for our journey, or should we do what we can to prepare ahead of time? What do we think about healing being a part of spreading Jesus's good news?

[Discover another time when Jesus sends his followers out two by two to tell others about him in Luke 10:1–24.]

DAY 15: JOHN THE BAPTIST
MARK 6:14–29

For John had been saying to Herod, "It is not lawful for you to have your brother's wife." (Mark 6:18)

We talked about John the Baptist's mission in Day 1. Now we see him a second and final time in the book of Mark, which records John's death.

Here's what happens:

Herod marries his brother's wife. Her name is Herodias. John the Baptist publicly criticizes Herod for committing this despicable act.

Herodias is angry. But the focus of her anger is surprising.

She could be mad at Herod for taking her from

her husband. But Herodias isn't. She could be mad at her first husband for not standing up to his brother and protecting her from Herod's selfish intent. Yet she is not.

Instead, she's angry at John the Baptist for his criticism of what Herod did. She holds a grudge. But this isn't an ordinary grudge. It's severe. She wants John to pay for what he said. She wants him to die. Yet she doesn't have the power to bring about John's death. She instead fuels her grudge.

Herod arrests John for what he said, but Herod doesn't kill him. Herod fears John and protects him from his wife's wrath. Despite the criticism John directed at him, Herod recognizes John as a righteous and holy man. Herod also likes to listen to John, even though what John says perplexes him.

When Herod has a birthday, he throws a lavish party in his own honor. He invites important people to the celebration. At the party, Herodias's daughter comes and dances before the crowd. We don't know if this is spontaneous or planned. We also don't know if this is the innocent dance of a child or a more suggestive strut of a young woman.

Regardless, her performance delights Herod and impresses his guests. He's so pleased that he promises to give her almost anything she wants. Not knowing what to say, the girl consults with her mother. Herodias knows exactly what to request. It's barbaric, and it's selfish. Through her daughter, she asks for the execution of John the Baptist, presenting his severed head on a platter as evidence.

Dismayed at what Herodias requested through her daughter, Herod follows through to avoid embarrassment in front of his guests. Even though he doesn't want to, he orders John's beheading.

In this story, we see that John the Baptist dies for speaking the truth.

We see Herod taking his brother's wife because he can and ordering John the Baptist's execution to avoid embarrassment.

Yet Herodias is the bigger culprit. Fueling her grudge, she uses her daughter to manipulate her husband into killing her nemesis.

What can we learn from the characters in this story? How can we apply it to our lives?

[Discover more about Herod's sin in Leviticus 18:16 and Leviticus 20:21.]

DAY 16: SUPERNATURAL POWER

MARK 6:30–56

They begged him to let them touch even the edge of his cloak, and all who touched it were healed. (Mark 6:56)

Because of the disciples' work in spreading the good news, so many people flock to Jesus that he and his disciples don't even have time to eat. vKnowing that they need some rest, they climb into their boat in search of a quiet place. Yet the people race there on foot and arrive before Jesus does.

Jesus won't enjoy the rest he'd hoped for. Instead, he teaches the people.

As the day nears its end, the people are hungry. The disciples want to send them away, but Jesus tells his followers to give the people something to eat. They can't. It would cost way too much money, surely far more than they have.

Jesus asks how much food is available. The report is five loaves of bread and two fish. With Jesus this is enough—more than enough. Jesus has the people sit. The disciples pass out what little food they have. Jesus miraculously multiplies it. There's enough to feed everyone as much as they want. They even gather leftovers. They feed five thousand men, along with women and children.

After everyone eats, Jesus sends his disciples out in the boat while he dismisses the people. Then he goes up the mountain to pray. At last he has the solitude he sought.

That night, his disciples in the boat encounter treacherous weather. They strain at the oars to control the boat. Just before dawn, they spot Jesus walking on the water. They're understandably scared of what they see—something that's humanly impossible. Jesus tells them to not be afraid. He climbs in the boat, and the wind dies down.

When they reach the other side, people recognize him and tell everyone that Jesus has arrived. The people bring all who are sick to Jesus. They beg him to let them touch the edge of his cloak. All who do are healed. The same thing happened before, which we covered in Day 13.

In today's passage, we see Jesus's supernatural power in three ways. First, he multiplies a meager meal to feed thousands. Then he defies nature when he walks on water and stills the raging sea. Last, he proves his mastery over illness by healing sick and injured people.

We will later see him do one more wondrous thing. He will die to save us.

Which of these stories about Jesus amazes us the most? Which is the hardest one for us to accept?

[Discover another time Jesus feeds thousands in Mark 8:1–13.]

DAY 17: JESUS CLARIFIES THE LAW
MARK 7:1–23

"You have let go of the commands of God and are holding on to human traditions." (Mark 7:8)

The religious leaders continue to look for ways to discredit Jesus. When they can't attack him, they attack his disciples. We covered one time in Day 7 when they accuse Jesus's disciples of working on the Sabbath because they pick a handful of grain to eat.

In today's passage they criticize the disciples again. It's because the disciples don't conform with their tradition of washing their hands. Though handwashing is a wise idea, the Old Testament doesn't command it. Instead, well-meaning people over the centuries added to what Scripture proclaimed. The ceremonial washing of hands was one such tradition.

Quoting Isaiah's prophecy, Jesus proclaims them hypocrites. Isaiah wrote that the people say the right things, but their hearts are distant. Their worship is in vain because they follow man-made rules (Isaiah 29:13).

Consider this with care. How does our worship today follow man-made rules?

Jesus succinctly declares, "You ignore God's commands to maintain your traditions."

Then the Teacher gives an example. Their customs allow them to disregard one of the Ten Commandments—to honor your father and mother —if they dedicate to God what they would've used for their parents. In this way, their customs push away God's command.

Now back to their custom of handwashing.

In God's perspective, what we put in our body does not defile us. Instead, it's what comes out that makes us unclean. In this way, Jesus proclaims all food as being clean. Yet he also details what makes us unclean, what defiles us.

It all starts from within, from our hearts. Out of our hearts come evil thoughts. These impure thoughts lead to sexual immorality, theft, murder, adultery, greed, malice, deceit, lewdness, envy, slander, arrogance, and folly. These all make us unclean; they cause us to fall short of God's exacting standards for right behavior.

As we skim through this lengthy list of twelve items, murder may jump out. Most of us have not committed murder. With this perspective, it's easy to dismiss the rest of the list as well. But we shouldn't. Slow down and read each item with care.

When have we wanted more than we need (greed)? When have we wanted what someone else had (envy)? Have we ever said something wrong about someone else (slander)? When have we been proud (arrogant)? When have we acted foolishly (folly)?

These are what defile us, not what we eat.

Though we all fall short of avoiding these twelve defiling actions, we need not worry about our status with God.

Jesus came to earth to show us a better way. He died as the ultimate payment for all the wrong things we have done and ever will do. This includes sexual immorality, theft, murder, adultery, greed, malice, deceit, lewdness, envy, slander, arrogance, and folly.

Though we should strive to avoid all twelve, we can take comfort in knowing that when we falter our Savior covers them all. Jesus makes us right with Father God, and we no longer need to be held captive to the commands of the Old Testament or the traditions of people.

Which of these twelve items do we struggle with the most? What customs or traditions do we have that we need to eliminate?

[Discover more about clean and unclean in Acts 10:28.]

DAY 18: TWO MORE HEALINGS
MARK 7:24–37

Then he told her, "For such a reply, you may go; the demon has left your daughter." (Mark 7:29)

Next Jesus goes to the area of Tyre. He enters a house and doesn't want anyone to know he's there. I suspect he wants to rest and pray, recharging himself for more ministry.

Yet he can't keep his presence a secret. A woman shows up, but she isn't Jewish. She's a foreigner—a Greek. An impure spirit controls her daughter. The woman implores Jesus to drive out the demon and restore her daughter to full health and right thinking.

It may surprise us when Jesus tells her, "No."

This is shocking, but he explains why. Jesus came to minister to his own people—the Jews. They are his focus—for now. Though he will later tell his disciples to go out into the world to tell everyone about him, right now he shares his good news only with the Hebrew people.

The Teacher communicates this indirectly. He implies he's there for the children (that is, God's chosen people) and she doesn't qualify. He hints that she's a dog.

Though his rebuff would offend me, it doesn't dissuade the woman. She makes a quick comeback, witty and astute. "Even the dogs eat the children's crumbs."

Affirming her logic and accepting her request, Jesus does as she asks. He sends her home with the assurance that the demon has left her daughter. When she arrives, her daughter is resting and freed.

Though the woman believed Jesus could heal her daughter, there's no mention of Jesus reacting because of her faith. It seems Jesus reacted because of her persistence.

Then Jesus travels to another city in the region. Some people bring him a man who is deaf and can hardly talk. They plead for Jesus to heal the man.

Though we might think Jesus should do this in public to ensure everyone witnesses his miraculous power, he doesn't. Taking the man aside, Jesus removes him from the crowd. But Jesus doesn't proclaim healing on the man. Instead, he does some strange things.

First, he puts his fingers in the man's ears. Then he spits and touches the man's tongue. He looks up into heaven, sighs deeply, and says, "Be opened." The man is healed; he can now hear and speak plainly.

Jesus tells the people to keep what he did a secret, to tell no one. But they don't. In fact, the more he implores them to be quiet, the more they want to talk about it.

For the deaf man, there's no mention of him having faith, either. But his friends who brought him to Jesus may have had a bit of faith. At least they held onto hope that Jesus might heal him. Otherwise, why would they bring the man to Jesus?

Regardless of the degree that faith played (or didn't play), Jesus restored the man's hearing.

What do these two healings teach us about faith? How can these stories encourage us when we feel our faith is weak?

[Discover more about healing faith in Mark 5:34 and Mark 10:52.]

DAY 19: BREAD AND YEAST
MARK 8:1–21

*His disciples answered, "But where in this remote place can
anyone get enough bread to feed them?" (Mark 8:4)*

Around this time, another large crowd
gathers. We don't know if they're there
to watch Jesus heal the sick or to hear
him speak. Perhaps it's both. Regardless, they've
been with him for three days and have eaten all
their food. They're hungry.

Gathering his disciples, Jesus shares his concern.

The disciples wonder where they can find
enough bread in such a remote place to feed everyone. It seems they've already forgotten Jesus super-

naturally feeding the five thousand men, which we covered in Day 16.

Jesus asks how many loaves of bread they have. This should certainly spark their memory about what happened before when they had five loaves. It does not. This time there are fewer people to feed and a bit more bread.

Just as before, Jesus tells the crowd to sit. He takes the seven loaves of bread, thanks God, and gives it to the disciples to distribute to the people. He also adds a few small fish to the meal.

Just as before, the people eat all they want and are full. Just as before, the disciples pick up the leftovers.

The Pharisees ask Jesus for a sign from heaven. It seems his miraculous feeding of more than four thousand people isn't enough for them. They want more.

Yet before we criticize the Pharisees too deeply for missing Jesus's supernatural power, we'll soon see his disciples struggle with this as well.

Leaving the crowd and the Pharisees behind, Jesus and his disciples leave in a boat. The Teacher has a cryptic warning for them. "Be careful," he says. "Watch out for the yeast of the Pharisees—and of Herod."

The disciples don't know what to make of this. They reason among themselves, trying to decipher the meaning behind Jesus's warning. They wrongly conclude that he's criticizing them because they only brought one loaf of bread, which isn't enough to feed everyone.

Jesus tries to reorient their perspective. "Why are you so concerned about not having enough bread? Remember all the leftovers we had after I fed the five thousand? What about the leftovers when I fed the four thousand? Why don't you understand that bread isn't an issue for me?"

Instead of thinking about the physical need to feed themselves, Jesus warns his disciples to guard against the spiritual influence—that is, the yeast— of the Pharisees.

Are we more concerned with physical pursuits or spiritual matters? Whose influence might we need to guard against?

[Discover more about the influence of yeast in Matthew 13:33, Luke 13:20–21, 1 Corinthians 5:6–8, and Galatians 5:7–10.]

DAY 20: DON'T TELL ANYONE
MARK 8:22–30

"But what about you?" [Jesus] asked. "Who do you say I am?" Peter answered, "You are the Messiah." (Mark 8:29)

When I think of Jesus healing people, I envision him laying his hand on them and proclaiming healing. Perhaps you do too. Sometimes Jesus just proclaims it. Yet in Day 18, when he heals a deaf man, Jesus does something different. He puts his fingers in the man's ears. Then Jesus spits and touches the deaf man's tongue. The man receives complete healing; he can hear and speak (Mark 7:31–37).

In today's passage, we read another unexpected

healing encounter. This time Jesus spits on the man's eyes before he places his hands on him. The man's sight is partially restored. Jesus does it again. The second time, the man's sight is fully restored.

In both instances, Jesus tells the healed men to not tell anyone about what happened. Why the secrecy? This is no way to let others know about his healing power and grow his following.

Later, as Jesus and his disciples leave, the Teacher asks them, "Who do people say I am?"

The disciples give him a quick list of common answers: John the Baptist, Elijah, or one of the prophets.

Then Jesus asks them, "What do you think?"

Quick-to-speak Peter is the first to answer. "You are the Messiah."

We might expect Jesus to tell his disciples to go forth and share Peter's bold statement of truth with everyone. He doesn't. Instead, he tells them to keep it a secret, to not let anyone know he's the Messiah.

Why? It seems he doesn't want everyone to know, that he wants to save only a few.

First, consider the psychology of the situation. If you tell someone not to do something—especially to not talk about something exciting—their first reaction would be to tell even more people. Telling them not to say anything may be more effective than instructing them to tell everyone.

Another consideration, however, is that Jesus may want to keep news of his healing and teaching from getting back to the religious leaders in Jerusalem—and to their Roman occupiers.

The religious leaders view Jesus as a danger to disrupt what little power and authority the Romans have given them. They want to keep what they have. As for their part, the Romans seek a manageable situation, which Jesus seems to destabilize. He's a threat to both groups.

Jesus knows he will die for the people's sins. The religious leaders will orchestrate it, and the Romans will carry it out. Yet to reach fruition, they cannot react prematurely. What if they were to just imprison Jesus? That would keep him from accomplishing the precise thing he came to do: die for our sins.

Do we keep the good news of Jesus a secret or do we tell everyone about him? What can we learn from the strange way Jesus heals these two men?

[Discover when Jesus later instructs his followers to tell everyone in Mark 16:15–18.]

DAY 21: GET BEHIND ME SATAN
MARK 8:31–38

But when Jesus turned and looked at his disciples, he rebuked Peter. "Get behind me, Satan!" he said. "You do not have in mind the concerns of God, but merely human concerns."
(Mark 8:33)

After healing the man, Jesus shares what will soon happen. And it's not what his followers expect or want.

Jesus says he'll suffer terribly. The religious leaders—the elders, chief priests, and legal scholars —will reject him. They'll kill him. But not to worry, because three days later, he'll rise from the dead.

This is a lot to take in.

The disciples don't want their teacher to die—

none of his supporters do. They want him to amass a following and grow their movement. They likely expect him to mount a military resistance against their Roman occupiers and free their nation from oppression.

This is one way to interpret the Old Testament prophecies about the coming Savior. And it's what most people expect will happen. But Jesus didn't come to save them from foreign occupation. He came to save them from their sinful actions. He didn't come to free them physically as much as to rescue them spiritually.

As we might expect, Peter responds first. He pulls Jesus aside and reprimands him. Imagine that, the student correcting the Teacher.

Jesus's response is both shocking and direct. "Get behind me, Satan!" Then Jesus explains that Peter—and the other disciples—hold the wrong view. God's perspective differs from theirs.

In saying this, however, Jesus isn't proclaiming that Peter is Satan.

Though Satan may have tempted Peter to say what he said, it's more likely the disciple said this on his own accord. A better understanding is that Satan uses Peter's words to tempt Jesus and discourage him from completing his mission. Satan already tried this once, which we covered in Day 2.

Having rebuked Peter, the Teacher calls the crowd to him. He teaches them that to be his disciple, they must set their personal needs aside, take up their cross—which implies sacrifice—and follow him.

Those who try to save their life—which is what Peter wanted Jesus to do—will lose it. But whoever gives their life for Jesus will save it.

How well are we doing at giving our life to Jesus? Do we see God's perspective or look at our life from a human point of view?

[Discover more about giving our life to Jesus in Matthew 19:29.]

DAY 22: I BELIEVE!

MARK 9:1–32

The boy's father exclaimed, "I do believe; help me overcome my unbelief!" (Mark 9:24)

Six days later, Jesus takes Peter, James, and John with him to ascend a mountain, with the other nine disciples remaining behind. There on the mountain, Jesus transfigures before them. It's an amazing supernatural experience. Then they descend the mountain to rejoin their group.

They arrive to find a large crowd gathered around the other nine disciples, who are arguing with the religious teachers. When the people see

Jesus, they stream toward him. He asks what the commotion is all about.

A man in the crowd answers. "An evil spirit possesses my son, and he can't talk. It's even tried to kill him. I asked your disciples to cast out the spirit. They tried but couldn't."

This news dismays Jesus. He calls them an unbelieving generation. We don't know if he's talking about his disciples or about the people gathered, but remember that in Day 14, Jesus sent his disciples out two by two. One thing they did was cast out demons. Why can't they do it now?

As Jesus and the father talk, the child has a convulsion.

In desperation, the dad looks at Jesus. "If you can, please help us."

"If I can?" Jesus asks. "Everything's possible if only you will believe."

The father immediately responds. "I believe. Help me with my unbelief."

Jesus rebukes the impure spirit, commanding it to leave the boy and never return.

As it departs, the spirit shrieks and shakes the boy violently. The boy falls; he appears dead. Some people think he is. But even if he's dead, this isn't an issue for Jesus. The Healer takes the boy by his hand and helps him stand.

Though the father had faith in Jesus's healing power, he also harbored doubts. But his struggle with faith didn't keep him from receiving what he wanted. He gave Jesus the faith he had and trusted Jesus to cover the rest.

When they're alone, the disciples ask Jesus why they couldn't exorcise the spirit.

His answer is direct—and convicting. "This kind can only come out by prayer."

When our faith waivers, do we cling to what we have and trust Jesus to cover our doubt? How often do we limit ourselves because of a lack of prayer?

[Discover more about faith in Acts 14:8–10, Hebrews 4:14, James 5:15, and Jude 1:3. Read about doubt in James 1:6 and Jude 1:22.]

BONUS CONTENT: THE TRANSFIGURATION

Then a cloud appeared and covered them, and a voice came from the cloud: "This is my Son, whom I love. Listen to him!" (Mark 9:7)

When Jesus, Peter, James, and John ascend the mountain, it's just the four of them. That's when Jesus transforms before them. His clothes dazzle in whiteness. Elijah and Moses—though both long dead—supernaturally appear. They talk with Jesus.

Peter wants to commemorate this unprecedented event. He offers to build them each a shrine or tabernacle in their honor.

Before Jesus responds, a bright cloud forms. The voice of Father God comes from the cloud. "This is my Son," he says. "I love him. Listen to what he says."

In one succinct declaration, God confirms Jesus as the Son of God, affirms Jesus's ministry, and commands the disciples to listen to him.

Elijah and Moses vanish. It's now just Jesus and his three disciples.

Does hearing God's audible voice about Jesus sound familiar? We covered this in Day 2. When Jesus begins his public ministry, he asks John the Baptizer to baptize him. As Jesus comes up from the water, a voice from heaven booms. "This is my Son. I love him and am pleased with him."

Peter, James, and John were not likely there when Jesus was baptized. They didn't hear the words of Father God confirming who Jesus was. Yet when Jesus transfigures before them on the mountain, they hear for themselves the words of Father God.

Until now, they've only had what Jesus said about himself to go on. Now they have confirmation in God's own voice, confirming Jesus is the Son of God.

Now they know for sure.

How might we have reacted if we saw Jesus—or anyone— transform before us? Do we think we can hear God speak audibly to us today?

[Discover another time God speaks aloud in Acts 9:1–9.]

DAY 23: WELCOME THE CHILDREN
MARK 9:33–50

"Whoever welcomes one of these little children in my name welcomes me; and whoever welcomes me does not welcome me but the one who sent me." (Mark 9:37)

To teach the disciples a lesson about how God views people, Jesus takes a small child in his arms. Looking at his disciples, he tells them, "Anyone who welcomes a child in my name welcomes me. By extension that person also welcomes my Father—the one who sent me."

Though God's view is different, in that day's culture, children had little value. This is not so with Jesus. He values children, both then and now.

Imagine us today when we embrace a child in

Jesus's name. It's as though we embrace our Savior. It's as though we embrace his Father too. What better way to show our love to God than to love children in his name. We should consider this imagery the next time—every time—we hug a child. We're in effect hugging our Lord too.

We should not stop them from coming to Jesus. God's kingdom belongs to them—to the children. We should bless them every chance we get (Mark 10:13–15).

As Jesus continues his teaching, he warns against anything we might do to cause one of his children to stumble. It would be better for that person to die. That's a harsh statement, but it shows us just how important children are to Jesus.

Though people can put their faith and trust in Jesus at any age, we see that the younger they are, the more likely they are to do it. Also, if we point our children to God, they will retain our teaching when they move into adulthood (Proverbs 22:6). This isn't a onetime event on our part, but an ongoing effort (Deuteronomy 6:7).

Just like children, we all need to come to God as a child. We must accept him with a childlike faith. As an adult, our intellect and our logic will only get in our way; it will hinder us from following him.

Instead, we must push human wisdom aside and embrace Jesus through a simple faith, like that of a child.

Recall the lesson in Day 18 when the Greek woman comes to Jesus for healing for her daughter. In his cryptic response, the Teacher says, "Let the children eat first" (Mark 7:27). In saying this Jesus implies the children of God. Back then this meant the Jewish people. Now it means us too.

When we follow Jesus, we become children of God.

How can we better welcome children in Jesus's name? What does it mean to be children of God?

[Discover more about being children of God in John 1:11–13, Romans 8:14–17, and Galatians 3:26.]

DAY 24: LEAVE IT ALL BEHIND
MARK 10:1–31

Then Peter spoke up, "We have left everything to follow you!"
(Mark 10:28)

A rich man runs up to Jesus and kneels before the Teacher. He asks a simple question: "What must I do to receive eternal life?"

Jesus refers him to some of the key commandments: do not murder, do not commit adultery, do not steal, and do not give false testimony. Another is to honor your father and mother. These are five of the Ten Commandments as found in the law of Moses (Exodus 20:12–16 and Deuteronomy 5:16–20).

Jesus's answer encourages the man.

"I've done all these things since I was a kid," the man says. He must have a smug satisfaction. He surely thinks he's in, that Jesus will affirm his right living as enough to qualify him to receive eternal life.

Not so.

Jesus looks at the man in love and tells him to do one more thing. "Give everything you have to the poor. Then come and follow me."

The man's expectations fall. He slinks away in sadness because he is very wealthy.

Then Jesus tells his disciples, "It's hard for rich people to enter the kingdom of God."

This shocks the disciples. They assumed righteous living would qualify them. They assumed rich people had an edge and received favor in their standing with God. Now they know that right living isn't enough to earn salvation, and money can't buy eternal life.

"How then can anyone be saved?" they ask.

"With men, it's impossible," Jesus states unequivocally. "But with God, all things are possible."

As expected, Peter reacts first. "We left everything to follow you."

Jesus lists things people may give up when they follow him. This includes their home, family, and possessions. Jesus promises they'll receive a hundredfold return in this world. Then they'll receive eternal life when they die.

Jesus's promise of a hundredfold return for what we give up when we follow him and share his good news may seem like hyperbole—an unrealistic outcome. Yet we might be better off to not think in physical terms but in spiritual.

Recall the parable of the sower (in Day 9) where a good seed produces a hundredfold return. As we invite people to follow Jesus, we might get a hundredfold return for the seeds we plant. Spiritually, they become our home, our family, and even our possessions. This is our reward in this world. Then we'll spend eternity with them in the next. This is even better,

Giving everything to Jesus and following him is what matters.

What are we trying to do to earn—or maintain—our salvation? What are we holding onto that keeps us from truly following Jesus?

[Discover more about putting the past behind us in Genesis 19:26 and Luke 9:62. Read Jesus's definition of family in Mark 3:33–34.]

DAY 25: BE A SERVANT

MARK 10:32–52

"Whoever wants to become great among you must be your servant." (Mark 10:43)

A passage we didn't cover in Day 23 was the disciples arguing about who was the greatest. Jesus tells them that to be first, they must be last, that they must have the mindset of a servant (Mark 9:33–35).

We return to this concept in today's reading. James and John ask Jesus for a favor.

"What is it?" the Teacher asks.

They have a ready answer. "When you come to power, we want to sit on your right side and your left."

It's a huge request, and Jesus tells them so. "Are you ready to endure all that I must endure?"

They insist they are.

"You will indeed endure much," Jesus says. "But it isn't up to me to grant who will sit on my left and my right. In fact, those places are reserved for others."

The remaining ten disciples are furious at James and John for their boldness and the audacity of their request.

But before another argument erupts, Jesus intercedes with a relevant teaching. He concludes it by saying, "Whoever wants to rise to be the greatest must be your servant. Whoever wants to be first must be a slave to all."

Then Jesus reminds them of the example he set for them. "I did not come for others to serve me, but for me to serve them. The ultimate way to serve them is for me to die as a ransom for their sins."

Jesus calls us to serve others, just as he did. We shouldn't expect others to wait on us, but for us to wait on them. We shouldn't presume on others to do our bidding for us, but to do theirs for them.

A friend once complained that his church offered no service opportunities. He and his family quietly found a new congregation that provided options to serve. They quickly got involved and began serving in various ways.

Not only is this an admirable attitude, but serving is also what Jesus did.

He didn't expect others to serve him (though some did). He looked for ways to serve them. Jesus taught them, healed them, and pointed them to the kingdom of God, all while expecting nothing in return.

In the end, he died for them—and for us—covering our many failures (our sins) to make us right with Father God and reconcile us to him. Jesus gave his life for us, so that we could live with him forever.

Jesus freely served others. We should do the same.

How can we more effectively serve others? When have we expected someone to serve us?

[Discover more about serving others in John 12:26, Romans 7:6, and Romans 14:17–18.]

DAY 26: A HOUSE OF PRAYER
MARK 11:1–19

[Jesus] said, "Is it not written: 'My house will be called a house of prayer for all nations'? But you have made it 'a den of robbers.'" (Mark 11:17)

Jesus rides into Jerusalem on a colt. People line the path and call out their praise. "Hosanna! Hosanna in the highest!" Jesus goes to the temple courts, looks around, and leaves. It's already late in the day; he and his disciples go to Bethany for the night.

The next morning, they return to Jerusalem. As they leave Bethany, Jesus spots a fig tree. He's hungry. He searches for figs among the foliage but finds nothing. Jesus curses the tree. "May no one ever eat your fruit again."

They reach Jerusalem, go to the temple and enter its courts. Merchants have set up shops. They're selling doves, which the people need for some of their required sacrifices. There are also money changers to help facilitate the transactions.

This enrages Jesus.

He drives out the merchants. He overturns their tables and benches. Then he guards the entrance and doesn't allow anyone to carry any more merchandise into the temple courts. In doing so, he stops all buying and selling.

Explaining his actions, Jesus teaches the people. He quotes the prophet Isaiah. "My house will be called a house of prayer for everyone" (Isaiah 56:7).

It isn't just a house of prayer for the Hebrew people. It's a house of prayer for everyone. This includes Gentiles (all who are not Jews). At least that's what Isaiah prophesied, even if his forward-looking statement has not yet occurred.

Jesus concludes with a passage from Jeremiah: "But you have turned it into a robbers' den" (Jeremiah 7:11). What a scathing rebuke.

The temple serves as the people's holy place,

their sanctuary where they go to encounter God. There they worship him and pray. At least that's the goal of many.

Yet Jesus sees the merchants selling in the temple courts as having corrupted that purpose. They turned it into a mercantile of greedy profiteers instead of keeping it as a holy place of worship. In effect, they desecrated God's holy temple.

That evening, Jesus and his disciples leave the city. When they return the next day, the fig tree Jesus cursed is dead.

With the story of Jesus chasing away the temple merchants within the story of the unproductive fig tree, we're right to ponder a connection between the two. Might the death of the tree with no fruit connect with worship that misses God's purpose? It, too, is dead and serves no function.

In what ways have we desecrated God's house? Though we can pray anytime, anywhere, do we treat church as a house of prayer?

[Discover more about prayer in Acts 1:14, Acts 2:42, Romans 12:12, Ephesians 6:18, Colossians 4:2, James 5:15–18, and 1 Peter 3:7.]

DAY 27: MOVE MOUNTAINS

MARK 11:20–33

"Whatever you ask for in prayer, believe that you have received it, and it will be yours." (Mark 11:24)

The disciples notice the fig tree Jesus cursed is dead, withered from its roots. Peter points this out. "Rabbi, did you see what happened to the fig tree?"

I'm sure Jesus was aware of it, likely from the moment he first uttered those words and long before the disciples realized what had happened.

Jesus tells them—and us—to have faith.

With faith—and the absence of doubt—anyone can command a mountain to throw itself into the sea. It will happen. This is what we refer to as a faith that moves mountains.

Jesus continues teaching.

"I tell you the truth," he says, "whatever you pray for and believe you have received it, it will happen."

Then Jesus adds a surprising conclusion to his teaching. "If you're praying and suddenly remember a grudge you have against anyone or ill intent you hold, forgive them. Then God will forgive your sins."

This makes it seem like forgiveness is conditional. In a way, it is. When Jesus taught his disciples how to pray, one line says, "Forgive us our debts as we have forgiven our debtors" (Matthew 6:12). This implies that if we withhold forgiveness from others, we're allowing God to withhold it from us.

Jesus confirms this immediately after the prayer (Matthew 6:14–15). It's critical that we forgive others if we expect to receive God's full forgiveness.

From today's passage in Mark, we see three insights about prayer.

First is to place our faith in God. In faith, we believe Jesus for the forgiveness of our sins and follow him. In faith, we pray that our Lord hears and answers our requests.

Second is to believe we've already received what we pray for. This is faith at its best; this is praying with a God-honoring confidence. There is no room for doubt if we expect to receive. Instead, we wholeheartedly believe we have it even before it happens.

Third, harboring unforgiveness hinders our prayers. We must forgive others if we are to receive what God wants to give us.

We approach God in prayer through faith, believing we've already received what we ask. As we do, we guard against holding onto unforgiveness. This hampers our relationship with our Lord.

If we worry that our faith is weak, we can be like the father in Day 22 and say "Lord, I believe; help me with my unbelief."

How do we rate our own faith? What should we do about it?

[Discover more about faith and prayer in James 5:13–18.]

DAY 28: THE TOP TWO
MARK 12:1–31

"Love the Lord your God with all your heart and with all your soul and with all your mind and with all your strength."
(Mark 12:30)

Mark 11 ends with the religious leaders questioning Jesus's authority. He smartly avoids giving them a direct answer. But if they're willing to consider what he says, they could rightly conclude that his authority comes from God (Mark 11:27–33).

Next, in today's passage, Jesus gives them a parable about wicked tenants. It's a teaching about the religious leaders and their kind over the centuries. It's a scathing rebuke of how they treated

God's prophets and how they will treat Jesus. They want to arrest him for what he said, but they don't; they're afraid of the crowd.

Later, the religious leaders try to trap Jesus into saying something inflammatory about paying taxes. He also deftly dodges this one. His teaching amazes the people.

Next, the Sadducees—who don't believe in the resurrection of the dead—ask Jesus a hypothetical question relating to it. Not only does Jesus confirm that resurrection is a reality, but he refutes their implication of marriage in the afterlife.

The religious leaders have now made four unsuccessful attempts to trap Jesus into saying something they can use against him. Now one of their teachers of the law—we might call him a theologian today—asks Jesus a question. "What's the most important commandment?"

This man not only wants Jesus to choose from among the Ten Commandments but also from the 613 other commands found in the law of Moses about what to do and not do. He also likely has in mind the other thousands of rules that developed over the centuries to help people rightly follow the 613 written commands.

It's a lot to choose from.

As is often the case with Jesus, he gives a surprising answer. Jesus doesn't give the man one command; he gives two. But the Teacher has a good reason.

The first is to love God. This is the greatest command of all. We are to love God with our whole heart, all our soul, our complete mind, and every bit of strength we have (Deuteronomy 6:5).

The second greatest command is to love others. We are to love our neighbor as much as we love ourselves (Leviticus 19:18).

Love God and love others. There are no greater commands than these two.

If we follow these two commandments fully in all that we do, we address all the other commands and well-meaning guidelines as well.

If we love others and don't love God, we miss the point. Yet if we claim to love God but don't love others, we are a liar (1 John 4:20).

We must love both God and others.

How can we love God more fully? What can we do to better love our neighbors?

[Discover more about the importance of love in 1 Corinthians 13:1–3.]

DAY 29: GOD'S PERSPECTIVE ON GIVING

MARK 12:32–44

"They all gave out of their wealth; but she, out of her poverty, put in everything—all she had to live on." (Mark 12:44)

After Jesus says that the two greatest commands are to love God and love others, the man affirms Jesus's answer. He repeats what Jesus said and adds that loving our neighbor is more important than all the burnt offerings and sacrifices put together.

Jesus affirms the man's wisdom. "You're so close to being part of God's kingdom." After this, no one dares ask Jesus anything else.

With no one plying him with questions, Jesus

gives the people another teaching. It's about the Messiah being both David's Lord and David's son. They listen to him in delight.

He next warns about the teachers of the law. They like to be recognized and receive respect. Yet they take homes from widows and make long, showy prayers. As such, they'll receive a more severe punishment. They should know better, but their actions prove otherwise.

Jesus then sits near the offertory and watches the people make their donations. We don't normally think of Jesus being a people watcher. He's typically a man of action. Yet he's waiting for an object lesson to present itself. It soon will.

Rich people come along and throw in large amounts. This isn't a quiet donation; it's one done for show. They want people to see how generous they are. Recall that Jesus just criticized the religious leaders for doing things for show. He also criticized them for taking advantage of widows.

That's when a widow walks up to make her donation. Mark notes she's not merely a widow, but a poor one—perhaps poorer than most. I doubt she wants anyone to see how little she gives, especially after the grandiose displays of the rich people who went before her. She likely goes last.

She puts in two small coins, not even worth a penny.

Jesus points this out to his disciples. "This poor widow gave more than all the others combined!" Then the Teacher explains. "They gave a fraction of their wealth. She gave 100 percent—all she had to live on."

The rich people will return home, knowing they still have plenty of money and need not be concerned. The poor widow will return home completely broke, knowing she'll need to depend on God for her future.

Do we give out of our wealth or our poverty? Do we depend on God or money for our future?

[Discover more about giving in 1 Chronicles 21:24, 1 Corinthians 16:1–4, and 2 Corinthians 8:2–5.]

DAY 30: WATCH OUT
MARK 13:1–31

Jesus said to them: "Watch out that no one deceives you."
(Mark 13:5)

The thirteenth chapter in the book of Mark contains a record of Jesus teaching about the end times. This is a challenging passage to read; it's hard to understand. It also may fill us with worry over the future.

But we shouldn't be concerned about what will happen and when it may occur. We know that whatever difficulties we may face on earth, we'll spend eternity in heaven with Jesus—at least we will if we follow him.

Jesus begins by talking about the destruction of the temple.

The disciples want to know when this will occur.

Historically, we know the temple is destroyed just a few decades after Jesus makes these remarks. Yet there's also a forward-looking element to Jesus's words, one that has not yet occurred but one day will. Since the direct fulfillment of this passage has already happened, we'll look at what is still to come.

Jesus says, "Make sure no one confuses you about the future." We shouldn't let someone who claims to be Jesus deceive us. Wars or even rumors of wars, of earthquakes and famine should not cause alarm. These only signal the beginning of the end.

Therefore, we must be on our guard. Bad things will happen. We can count on it. Jesus says so. We'll face persecution. But this will also give us the opportunity to tell others about Jesus.

Before the end occurs, all the nations will hear of Jesus's good news. This isn't just some countries but all of them, every single one.

This means that before our world ends, the good news about Jesus will go out to every country. As long as there are unreached people groups, the end cannot yet occur.

Jesus also says that for our sake, God will cut those days short. Otherwise, we wouldn't survive.

Jesus warns of false messiahs and false prophets. Again, he tells us to be on guard.

When the end comes, the sun will go dark, the moon will fade, and the stars will fall. We'll see the Son of Man—that is, Jesus—coming in the clouds with power and glory. He'll send his angels to gather his followers.

For those of us who believe in him, what a glorious day that will be.

What is our attitude about the end of the world? Do we fear the future or trust God with it?

[Discover more about God's perspective of the end in 2 Peter 3:9.]

DAY 31: THE END IS NEAR
MARK 13:32–37

"Therefore keep watch because you do not know when the owner of the house will come back—whether in the evening, or at midnight, or when the rooster crows, or at dawn."
(Mark 13:35)

I n his teaching about the end of time, Jesus has already warned us twice to stay on guard, to watch for that day. Though he's given us a general explanation of when it will come, he plainly states that no one knows exactly when. Not the angels in heaven, and not him. Only Papa knows.

Now Jesus says a third time to be on our guard. He repeats this instruction to make sure we don't miss it.

Be on guard! Remain alert. Since no one knows when the world will end, we must be ever watching.

If the Bible says no one knows, why do some preachers make audacious predictions? It's impossible, yet they try anyway. I'm not sure if this is out of arrogance of who they are or ignorance over what the Bible says.

Yes, we need to be ready, but we don't know when the end will occur. So let's stop trying to figure out what we can't know and instead focus on doing what we already know: Jesus told us to be ever vigilant, to be on high alert and watch for the end. We must remain on guard.

Paul will later teach that the end will come as unexpectedly as a thief in the night, but this shouldn't surprise us. Until that day occurs, we should continue to encourage one another and build each other up (1 Thessalonians 5:1–11).

The apostle John, recording the words of Jesus, repeats this metaphor of Jesus's return coming unexpectedly like a thief. We will be blessed if we stay awake and remain ready for his return (Revelation 16:15).

This will be as it was in the days of Noah. He and his family were ready; the other people were blissfully unaware that destruction awaited. Aboard the ark, Noah and his family survived; everyone else died in the deluge (Genesis 7:21–23).

This is also just as with the people in the city of Sodom. Lot and his daughters fled destruction; no one else survived. Lot and his daughters lived; everyone else died—even Lot's wife perished when she looked back at all she was leaving behind (Genesis 19:12–29).

May we keep watch, be alert, and remain on guard as we wait for the day of Jesus's return. May he arrive to find us ready.

What should we do to keep watch and remain on guard? How should we react when someone predicts when the world will end?

[Discover more about the end—and what happens next—in Revelation 22.]

DAY 32: THE LORD'S SUPPER
MARK 14:1–26

"This is my blood of the covenant, which is poured out for many." (Mark 14:24)

Jesus continues to move toward his sacrificial death on our behalf; it is but days away. A woman anoints his head with expensive oil, which Jesus proclaims as a beautiful act that prepares his body for burial. I'm sure none of the people knew what he was talking about then, but we certainly do now.

Two days later, Jesus sends a pair of disciples into the city to prepare for their Passover celebration. He gives them some cryptic instructions.

Once in the city, they're to look for a man

carrying a jar of water. They should follow him. When he reaches his destination, they're to say to the owner of the house, "The Teacher wants to know where the guestroom is so he can eat Passover with his disciples." The man will take them to a room furnished and ready. That's where they're to prepare the Passover meal.

Moses instituted Passover as a family celebration done at home, but Jesus's family isn't there. They're back where he grew up. So are his disciples' families. Yet, as Jesus already said, those who do God's will are his family (Mark 3:34–35). This includes his disciples. In the absence of his biological family, it's fitting that Jesus will spend Passover with his spiritual family and they with him.

The headings added to some Bibles for this passage call it "The Last Supper." Although it will in fact be Jesus's last supper before his arrest, it's the first supper for those of us who follow him.

Today this meal goes by various names—the Lord's Supper, Holy Communion, and the Eucharist—even though these last two labels aren't found in the Bible. Regardless of what we call it, it's when Jesus takes the tradition of the Passover meal and turns it into a celebration of his sacrificial death.

Passover remembers God delivering the people from their physical bondage to slavery, while Communion remembers Jesus delivering us from our spiritual bondage to sin.

As they eat their meal, Jesus takes a loaf of bread. He thanks Papa for it. He breaks it and gives it to his disciples to eat. Then he says, "This is my body."

Next Jesus takes a cup and gives thanks for it too. He gives it to them, and they drink. He says, "My blood is a new covenant, poured out for many."

Then they sing a song and walk to the Mount of Olives. Though the disciples don't know what's about to happen, Jesus does. So do we.

We should remember this each time we take Communion.

What does Communion mean to us today? How can we better align our practice of the Lord's Supper with what Jesus implemented and the Passover celebration it's based on?

[Discover more about this solemn celebration in 1 Corinthians 11:23–26.]

BONUS CONTENT: JESUS ANOINTED

"She poured perfume on my body beforehand to prepare for my burial." (Mark 14:8)

Two days before Jesus celebrates the Passover meal with his disciples, he's eating at the home of Simon the Leper. Since the homeowner has leprosy, that means he's not there. He can't. He must isolate himself from society; the law requires it. But his family is there. So are other guests and Jesus's disciples.

During the meal, a woman approaches Jesus. She holds a jar of expensive perfume; it's pure nard. Breaking the jar open, she pours the entire contents over his head.

Some people criticize her for wasting something so valuable. They think she should have sold the perfume and given the money to the poor.

In their minds, the woman wasted it.

In her mind, she gave Jesus the most extravagant gift she could. She had no greater way to express her love than to give him her expensive perfume, which was worth more than a year's wage.

Jesus doesn't criticize her; he defends her. He celebrates what she did. She gave him what she could. She prepared him for burial. Then he adds a most delightful promise. "Everyone who hears about my good news throughout the world will know what she has done."

That's exactly what happened.

What generous gift can we offer to Jesus? How can this woman's love and generosity inspire us to do more for our Savior?

[Discover more about anointing in John 19:39–40, 2 Corinthians 1:21–22, Hebrews 1:9, and James 5:14.]

DAY 33: JESUS'S PRAYER

MARK 14:27–42

"Abba, Father," he said, *"everything is possible for you. Take this cup from me. Yet not what I will, but what you will."*
(Mark 14:36)

When they arrive at the Mount of Olives, Jesus selects Peter, James, and John to go with him. He leaves the other nine disciples in the garden of Gethsemane, telling them to sit there and wait. (Nonbiblical sources say the garden of Gethsemane is at the base of the Mount of Olives.)

This isn't the first time Jesus singles out Peter, James, and John for a special experience, leaving the other nine disciples with nothing to do but wait.

This also happened at his transfiguration (see the bonus content after Day 22). Given that something extraordinary happened then, the three disciples must be expectant this time as well.

When they ascend the mount, sorrow fills Jesus. He's troubled. He tells his three companions, "I'm overwhelmed. Keep watch with me as I pray."

He pours out his distress to Papa. At one point, Jesus asks God for a reprieve—that he won't have to die—even though that was the plan all along.

But he's quick to add an addendum, confirming he'll do whatever his Father wants.

I wonder if Jesus recalls the test God gave Abraham, commanding the patriarch to kill his son Isaac (Genesis 22:1–19). Just as Abraham prepares to plunge the knife into his son in total obedience, God calls out. "Wait!"

Then God provides an alternate sacrifice, a substitute. God spares Isaac.

I wonder if Jesus hopes God will again say, "Wait" and provide a substitute sacrifice or a different solution.

This time God the Father won't. Jesus willingly accepts that he must die as a once-and-for-all way to reunite us with Father God. He will die instead of us; he will take our punishment on himself.

When Jesus finishes his prayer, he returns to Peter, James, and John. Though he asked them to keep watch as he prayed, they faltered. They fell asleep.

When he needed them the most, they failed him.

Jesus gives them a second chance. He tells them to pray that they won't give in to the temptation to sleep. "Though your spirit may be willing," he says, "your flesh is weak."

He moves away and prays a second time. Again he returns and finds them asleep. Leaving them to their slumber, Jesus prays a third time.

Then he wakes them. He's about to be arrested.

When have we failed Jesus? How can we pray to avoid giving in to temptation?

[Discover more about Jesus's sacrifice in Hebrews 7:27 and Hebrews 10:1–18.]

DAY 34: DESERTING JESUS
MARK 14:43–52

Then everyone deserted him and fled. (Mark 14:50)

Before Jesus celebrated the Passover meal with his disciples, he predicted one of them would betray him. So hideous this disloyalty, it would be better if that person had never been born (Mark 14:17–21). Though Jesus didn't identify which disciple would do this, we'll soon find out.

With Jesus having just awoken Peter, James, and John from their slumber, Judas approaches. He's the betrayer. A crowd follows him. They're armed with swords and clubs. The mob is there on behalf of the religious leaders: the chief priests, the teachers of the law, and the elders.

Though the religious leaders determined that Jesus must die, none of them are there to take him. They're content to let other people do their wicked work for them. This will keep them smugly distant from Jesus's death, even though they're orchestrating it.

Judas walks up to Jesus and kisses him. This prearranged signal lets the mob know who to go after. They seize Jesus and arrest him.

One of Jesus's followers whips out his sword and starts swinging. He lops off the ear of the high priest's servant. Given this man's status as a servant, he's likely present because his master ordered him to take part. He probably doesn't even want to be there.

Jesus, however, seems quite calm. "Am I leading a rebel army," he asks, "that you need to come here with weapons to arrest me? You could've easily done that any day in the temple courts."

Just as Jesus had predicted Judas's betrayal, after the Passover meal, Jesus foretold that all his disciples would desert him. Each of them would fall away and scatter. Peter asserted he would not. But Jesus disagreed, telling him that before the next morning,

Peter would deny Jesus three times. Peter adamantly insisted he would not. The others said the same thing (Mark 14:27–31).

With the mob having apprehended Jesus, everyone deserts him. They all run away, doing exactly what Jesus said they would do.

May we never betray Jesus like Judas did.

May we never abandon Jesus, like his disciples did, when we should take a stand.

If we have ever denied Jesus, what must we do to move beyond our mistake? How can we best prepare to take a stand for Jesus and not flee in fear?

[Discover more about the word *deny* in Mark 8:34 and 1 John 2:22.]

BONUS CONTENT: MARK REFERENCES THE OLD TESTAMENT

"Every day I was with you, teaching in the temple courts, and you did not arrest me. But the Scriptures must be fulfilled."
(Mark 14:49)

Though most people focus on the New Testament—and especially the life of Jesus—this doesn't mean the Old Testament lacks merit. Through the Old Testament Scriptures, we can better appreciate Jesus and what he came to do.

Here are the passages in the book of Mark that connect with the Old Testament. Some of these verses give us Jesus's own words as he teaches from Scripture.

- Mark 1:2 quotes Malachi 3:1.
- Mark 1:3 quotes Isaiah 40:3
- Mark 4:12 summarizes Isaiah 6:9–10.
- Mark 7:7 references Isaiah 29:13.
- Mark 7:10 quotes from Exodus 20:12 and Deuteronomy 5:16.
- Mark 7:10 also quotes Exodus 21:17 and Leviticus 20:9.
- Mark 9:48 quotes Isaiah 66:24.
- Mark 10:6 refers to Genesis 1:27.
- Mark 10:8 quotes from Genesis 2:24.
- Mark 10:19 quotes from Exodus 20:12–16 and Deuteronomy 5:16–20.
- Mark 11:9 paraphrases Psalm 118:25–26.
- Mark 11:17 references Isaiah 56:7 and Jeremiah 7:11.
- Mark 12:10–11 quotes Psalm 118:22–23.
- Mark 12:26 alludes to Exodus 3:6.
- Mark 12:29–30 quotes Deuteronomy 6:4–5.
- Mark 12:31 quotes Leviticus 19:18.
- Mark 12:36 quotes Psalm 110:1.
- Mark 13:14 references Daniel 9:27; 11:31; 12:11.

- Mark 13:25 references Isaiah 13:10; 34:4.
- Mark 14:7 quotes from Deuteronomy 15:11.
- Mark 14:27 quotes Zechariah 13:7.
- Mark 15:34 quotes Psalm 22:1.

How do we view the Old Testament? Why does Jesus teach from it?

[Discover more about Jesus fulfilling the Old Testament in Matthew 5:17.]

DAY 35: I AM
MARK 14:53–65

Again the high priest asked him, "Are you the Messiah, the Son of the Blessed One?" "I am," said Jesus. (Mark 14:61–62)

Having seized Jesus, the mob delivers him to the religious leaders as instructed. The high priest, all the chief priests, the elders, and the teachers of the law have all gathered. They've come together for one purpose. Their singular goal is to get rid of Jesus; they want to kill him. That will end his threat to their rule and the limited authority granted them by their Roman occupiers.

Peter follows at a distance. Though he abandoned Jesus along with the other disciples, just as Jesus said they would, Peter likely remembers his pledge to never leave Jesus. By trailing behind, this may be Peter's way of trying to make up for fleeing in fear.

The religious governing body—the Sanhedrin —seeks evidence to justify executing Jesus. But they can't find it. Many false witnesses testify, but their testimonies contradict one another. Others come forward and misquote Jesus, but they can't even agree on that.

At last, the high priest asks Jesus to defend himself. Jesus remains silent. The high priest tries a second time. He asks Jesus, "Are you the Messiah, the Son of God?"

Having been asked a direct question by the high priest, Jesus replies. "I am."

Not only does Jesus answer the high priest, but his wording carries a secondary meaning that all those who hear him would not miss.

Centuries earlier, Moses encountered God through a bush that was on fire but did not burn up (Exodus 3:1–14). God spoke to Moses from the bush. They have a lengthy conversation about what God wants Moses to do. He's supposed to go to his people and free them from captivity.

Moses hesitates. He has a question for God. "When the people ask me the name of who sent me, what should I say?"

"I AM WHO I AM," God tells Moses. "Tell my people, 'I AM has sent me to you.'"

I AM is God's name. By Jesus saying to the high priest, "I am," everyone there rightly sees him as equating himself to God.

Then Jesus gives them more damning evidence. He says, "You will see the Son of Man sitting at God's right hand in heaven."

By using the word *will*, Jesus gives them a future-focused reality. He *will* one day rule with God in heaven.

The religious leaders are aghast at Jesus's own admission. They accuse him of blasphemy. By his own testimony, they convict him, condemning him to death.

What is our testimony about Jesus? When have we acted like these religious leaders and wrongly condemned someone?

[Discover more about the great I am in Isaiah 48:12, John 6:35, John 8:12, and John 14:6.]

DAY 36: PETER FALTERS
MARK 14:66–72

Then Peter remembered the word Jesus had spoken to him: "Before the rooster crows twice you will disown me three times." And he broke down and wept. (Mark 14:72)

L et's review. Peter pledged he would never leave Jesus and was even willing to die with him. But Peter abandons Jesus, along with everyone else. We covered this in Day 34. Then, as if trying to correct his error, Peter follows the throng as they take Jesus to the Sanhedrin for a sham of a trial. We covered this in Day 35.

Now Peter moves closer to the drama. He's near where the Sanhedrin meet, waiting in the courtyard. I'm sure he hopes no one will notice him, but he wants to remain near Jesus. In that moment, this may be the best way he can support his master.

One of the high priest's servants walks by. She sees Peter warming himself by the fire. She scrutinizes him. "You were also with him," she states.

Peter denies it. "I don't know him or even understand what you're talking about." He retreats to the courtyard gate.

Seeing him there, the servant girl tells other people. "This guy is one of them."

Again, Peter denies any affiliation with Jesus.

Then others standing near Peter implicitly agree with the servant. They say, "You're from Galilee. Surely, you're one of his followers."

Peter calls down curses on himself if he's lying and swears he isn't. "I don't even know this man."

Then a rooster crows, triggering Peter's memory of Jesus's warning. He has now denied his Savior three times, just as Jesus said he would.

It's bad enough to have done it once. Twice is worse. But denying he even knows Jesus a third time adds emphasis to his claim. It confirms it.

Ironically, earlier that same day, Peter pledged his support to Jesus, professing his willingness to die with him (Mark 14:31).

For most people, admitting we *know* Jesus is a simple thing to do.

Yet a life-and-death situation confronted Peter: Say "yes" and he too could die with Jesus. Or say "no" and avoid further scrutiny, saving himself from what would soon befall his Master.

In the momentous pressure of the moment, Peter gives in to his fear and says "no." He asserts he doesn't know Jesus.

In some parts of the world, admitting we follow Jesus can result in suffering and possibly death. How well would we do in those circumstances?

Would we give in or be bold, regardless of the consequences?

Beyond the literal meaning of this story, there's a more profound supernatural element. It carries the opposite outcome.

In a spiritual sense, when we say yes to Jesus, we will live with him forever; saying no leads to death.

May we profess to knowing Jesus.

Do we truly know Jesus? Have we told others about him?

[Discover more about professing Jesus in Romans 10:10, Hebrews 4:14, and Hebrews 13:15.]

DAY 37: JESUS MOCKED AND KILLED

MARK 15:1–32

"Let this Messiah, this king of Israel, come down now from the cross, that we may see and believe." (Mark 15:32)

When we think of the suffering Jesus endured when he died on the cross for all the wrong things we've done, we often focus on his physical suffering: Of him being whipped and beaten. Of having spikes driven through his hands and feet. Of him straining to breathe and suffocating in immense pain and great agony.

Yet Jesus's suffering on our behalf wasn't merely physical. There was an emotional element, too, along with the spiritual gravity of the situation.

Having determined that Jesus must die for claiming to be God, the religious leaders have a problem. They don't have the power to execute anyone. Only their Roman occupiers can do that. They send Jesus to Pilate. As the Roman authority in the area, he can order someone's death.

Pilate knows the religious leaders are jealous of Jesus and want to get rid of him. Pilate tries to free the innocent man, but the religious leaders stir up a mob to demand Jesus's crucifixion. Pilate gives in to satisfy the crowd and avoid a riot. He has Jesus flogged and orders his execution.

The soldiers lead Jesus away. They want to have some fun at his peril. They dress him in a purple robe and fashion a crown made of thorns. Placing it on his head, they likely do so with as much force as they can to cause as much pain as possible.

Then they mock him by pretending to worship him. They hit him and spit on him. They kneel before him, feigning to pay homage. After tiring of their sport to humiliate Jesus, they lead him away to kill him.

Jesus is so weak that he can't even drag his own cross to the site of his execution. The soldiers force another man to do this for him. They even take

Jesus's clothes and cast lots—as if playing a game—
to see who should win them.

Next to him, the soldiers crucify two rebels.
They use their last moments of life to insult Jesus.
The people who walk by scream insults at him too.
They taunt Jesus to get down off the cross and save
himself.

Even the religious leaders mock Jesus among
themselves. They acknowledge that despite him
saving others, he's unable to save himself. "If he's
really the Messiah, let him prove it by climbing
down from the cross. When we see it, we'll believe!"

Aside from the physical and emotional suffering
Jesus endures as he dies for us, the spiritual impact
is even worse. The shame of all the sins, for all
people, throughout all time, piles on him at that
moment. He dies in our place for our mistakes.

Yet because Jesus dies, those who believe in him
will live. We have eternal life. That eternal life starts
the moment we follow Jesus and continues into
heaven after we die.

*When have we last thanked Jesus for all he endured to save
us? What can we do to better show our appreciation for what
he did?*

[Discover more about death in Romans 6:23, 2 Timothy 1:9–10, and Hebrews 2:9.]

DAY 38: AN UNEXPECTED TESTIMONY

MARK 15:33–41

*When the centurion, who stood there in front of Jesus, saw
how he died, he said, "Surely this man was the Son of God!"*
(Mark 15:39)

J esus hangs on the cross. It's noon. The sky
turns dark. Three hours later, Jesus cries out
in distress. "God, why have you left me
alone?"

How can we interpret this? Did Father God
desert Jesus, just like all his disciples?

One thought is that for Jesus to bear all our sins
completely, he must do it alone. The Father can't
help him endure his struggle. It's Jesus's mission and

his alone. In doing so, he becomes the ultimate sacrifice to end all sacrifices.

There's also the thought that holy God can't bear to look at all the sin Jesus carries at that moment. Papa must turn away and not see it. In that instant, Jesus is alone.

Then Jesus breathes his last and dies. It is finished.

The curtain in the temple rips in two. Why is this detail important?

In the Old Testament, the people see the temple as God's dwelling place on earth. Therefore, to approach God, they had to go to the temple. They worship God there and no place else. God commands it.

In the temple hangs a thick veil—a heavy curtain. It separates the temple's inner sanctum where God lives—the Most Holy Place—from the regular people, even the priests. The only person who can enter the Most Holy Place is one specially selected priest and then only once a year.

When Jesus breathes his final breath, the veil in the temple rips in two. This symbolically gives us direct access to God, with no priest needed to act as an intermediary. Note that the veil tears from top to bottom—from heaven to earth—showing that God initiated it.

Now, through faith in Jesus, we may approach God directly, freely, and with confidence. The veil is gone. We have no need for a middleman to act as our liaison to God.

The centurion overseeing Jesus's execution witnesses Jesus's death. Though he isn't Jewish and doesn't share their beliefs, he comprehends what just occurred. He says, "This man was most surely God's Son."

The centurion wasn't living in expectation that God would send a Savior to liberate his people from their slavery to sin. He didn't know all the Old Testament prophecies that looked forward to Jesus's saving work on our behalf. He only knew what he saw. What he saw was Jesus, the Son of God, die for us.

This is the centurion's testimony about Jesus.

What is our testimony about Jesus? What does his sacrificial death mean to us?

[Discover more about what Jesus's death means in 1 Corinthians 6:19–20, Ephesians 3:12, and 1 Peter 2:4–9.]

DAY 39: JESUS RESURRECTS
MARK 15:42–MARK 16:8

"Don't be alarmed," he said. "You are looking for Jesus the Nazarene, who was crucified. He has risen! He is not here. See the place where they laid him." (Mark 16:6)

Jesus is dead. But this won't provide the resolution the religious leaders wanted. Jesus's influence will only grow, heightening their concerns. Their problem isn't going away; it's going to get worse.

A leading member of the Council (the Sanhedrin) is Joseph of Arimathea. Yet, unlike most of the Council, Joseph lives in expectation of the coming of God's kingdom.

Not wanting Jesus's body to hang in disrespect on the cross over the Sabbath, Joseph rushes to Pilate, asking for permission to remove Jesus's body and bury it. He hurries to finish his task before the Sabbath begins, when he must rest and can't do any work. He places Jesus's body in a rock-hewn tomb, blocking the entrance with a huge stone.

After the Sabbath, Mary Magdalene and some of her friends go to the tomb. They want to prepare Jesus's body for a proper interment, which Joseph apparently didn't have time to complete before the Sabbath began.

The women reach the tomb. To their amazement, the stone sealing its entrance has been rolled away. Curious, they walk inside the cavern. There sits a young man, wearing a white robe. He's likely an angel. His presence concerns them.

"Don't be afraid," he says. "The crucified body of Jesus isn't here. He's risen from the dead. Tell his disciples!"

Some Christians focus on Jesus's sacrificial death, dying in our place for the wrong things we have done. This atones for our sins and makes us right with Father God. It is proper to memorialize Jesus's death.

Other Christians focus on Jesus's resurrection from the grave. This proves his mastery over death. If death can't hold him, it won't hold us either—providing we follow Jesus. It is right to celebrate Jesus's resurrection.

Jesus's sacrificial death alone isn't enough. Neither is his resurrection. The two go together. We must celebrate both. A sacrificial death without resurrection accomplishes little. Yet without the sacrificial death, resurrection isn't needed.

Connecting these two events is Jesus's burial. It proves he died, which both his sacrifice and his resurrection require. We have the young man's—the angel's—testimony (Mark 16:5–6). Mary Magdalene and her friends witnessed Jesus's death (Mark 15:40, 47), the centurion confirmed it (Mark 15:39, 44–45), and Joseph of Arimathea acted upon it (Mark 15:46).

Our salvation and our eternity require both Jesus's death and resurrection. May we balance them and embrace both.

May we give equal attention to Jesus's sin-saving sacrifice and his life-saving resurrection.

Are we more in awe of Jesus's sacrifice or his resurrection? What can we do to better balance our appreciation of both?

[Discover more about Jesus's death, burial, and resurrection in 1 Corinthians 15:3–7.]

DAY 40: LAST INSTRUCTIONS

MARK 16:9–20

He said to them, "Go into all the world and preach the gospel to all creation." (Mark 16:15)

Not all manuscripts of the book of Mark contain this concluding section, but that doesn't mean we should dismiss it. It's an important epilogue, needed to wrap up Mark's account of Jesus. Maybe Mark later added this addendum. If not him, then some of his successors did. This need not concern us, for these words align with the other three biblical accounts of Jesus's life.

Just prior to this clarifying text, verse 8 ends our story abruptly, with the women being afraid to share the good news of Jesus's resurrection with the disciples as the angel instructed. Yet we know this isn't the end. The epilogue corrects this premature conclusion by detailing what happens next.

Initially, the women may have been afraid to tell anyone—first because it seemed impossible and second because that culture didn't value a woman's testimony. But Mary Magdalene's reluctance is temporary.

Jesus appears to Mary. She goes to his followers who are mourning. She tells them the good news, yet they don't believe her.

Then Jesus appears to two of his followers walking down the road. They also tell the disciples, but the disciples don't believe them either.

Finally, Jesus appears to the eleven remaining disciples. He chastises them for their lack of faith and not believing the witnesses he sent to them.

Then he commissions them to tell others about him. They're to go throughout the world and proclaim the good news of him to everyone. This isn't just a message for the people who live in Judea. It's not just a message for the Hebrew people—the Jews. It's for everyone, in all places. Jesus wants the entire world to know about him.

Jesus promises that whoever believes and is baptized will be saved. But the unbelievers will not.

What these two scenarios don't cover are people who believe but aren't baptized. What's their eternal outcome? The legalistic response suggests they're out. Yet God's grace suggests they're in.

After all, believing is what matters (John 3:16 and Romans 10:9).

Jesus also gives five signs that will accompany those who believe: they will drive out demons, speak in tongues, handle snakes, be safe from drinking deadly poison, and heal the sick.

Though this list may be a challenging one for us to accept—especially the snakes and poison parts—the last line in the book of Mark confirms that this happened.

The disciples went as Jesus said. They preached everywhere, as Jesus said. He went with them and confirmed the good news about him through signs.

Yet we should not get bogged down by this specific list of signs. Instead, we must obey the central tenet of Jesus's instruction: Tell everyone about him.

What are we doing to tell others about Jesus? If we can't go throughout the world, how can we support those who do?

[Discover more about telling others of Jesus's good news in Acts 1:8 and 2 Peter 1:16–18.]

If you liked *Mark Bible Study*, please leave a review online. Your review will help others discover this book and encourage them to read it too.

Thank you.

BOOKS IN THE 40-DAY BIBLE STUDY SERIES

Which book do you want to read next in the 40-Day Bible Study Series?

- Dear Theophilus (the Gospel of Luke, formerly That You May Know)
- Acts Bible Study (formerly Tongues of Fire)
- Isaiah Bible Study (formerly For Unto Us)
- Dear Theophilus, Minor Prophets (formerly Return to Me)
- Dear Theophilus, Job (formerly I Hope in Him)
- Living Water (John)
- Love Is Patient (1 and 2 Corinthians)

- Revelation Bible Study
- Love One Another (1, 2, and 3 John)
- Run with Perseverance (Hebrews)
- James and Jude Bible Study
- Matthew Bible Study
- 1 & 2 Peter Bible Study

FOR SMALL GROUPS, SUNDAY SCHOOL, AND CLASSES

Mark Bible Study makes an ideal eight-week Bible study discussion guide for small groups, Sunday School, and classes. To prepare for the conversation, read one chapter of this book each weekday, Monday through Friday.

- Week 1: read 1 through 5.
- Week 2: read 6 through 10.
- Week 3: read 11 through 15.
- Week 4: read 16 through 20.
- Week 5: read 21 through 25.
- Week 6: read 26 through 30.
- Week 7: read 31 through 35.
- Week 8: read 36 through 40.

When you get together, discuss the questions at the end of each chapter. The leader can use all the questions to guide your discussion or pick which ones to focus on.

Before you begin, pray as a group. Ask for Holy Spirit insight and clarity.

As you consider each chapter's questions:

- Look for how this can grow your understanding of the Bible.
- Evaluate how this can expand your faith perspective.
- Consider what you need to change in how you live your lives.

End by asking God to help apply what you've learned.

May God bless you as you read and study his Word.

IF YOU'RE NEW TO THE BIBLE

Each entry in this book contains Bible references. These can guide you if you want to learn more. If you're not familiar with the Bible, here's an overview to get you started, give some context, and minimize confusion.

First, the Bible is a collection of works written by various authors over several centuries. Think of the Bible as a diverse anthology of godly communication. It contains historical accounts, poetry, songs, letters of instruction and encouragement, messages from God sent through his representatives, and prophecies.

Most versions of the Bible have sixty-six books grouped into two sections: The Old Testament and the New Testament. The Old Testament contains thirty-nine books that precede and anticipate Jesus. The New Testament includes twenty-seven books and covers Jesus's life and the work of his followers.

The reference notations in the Bible, such as Romans 3:23, are analogous to line numbers in a Shakespearean play. They serve as a study aid. Since the Bible is much longer and more complex than a play, its reference notations are more involved.

As already mentioned, the Bible is an amalgam of books, or sections, such as Genesis, Psalms, or Matthew. These are the names given to them, over time, based on the piece's author, audience, or purpose.

In the 1200s, each book was divided into chapters, such as Acts 2 or Psalm 23. In the 1500s, the chapters were further subdivided into verses, such as John 3:16. Let's use this as an example.

The name of the book (John) appears first, followed by the chapter number (3), a colon, and then the verse number (16). Sometimes called a chapter-verse reference notation, this helps people quickly find a specific text regardless of their version of the Bible.

Although the goal was to place these chapter and verse divisions at logical breaks, they sometimes seem arbitrary. Therefore, it's good practice to read what precedes and follows each passage you're studying. The text before or after it may contain relevant insights into the portion you're exploring.

Here's how to look up a specific passage in the Bible based on its reference: Most Bibles contain a table of contents, which gives the page number for the beginning of each book. Start there. Locate the book you want to read, and turn to that page. Then flip forward to the chapter you want. Last, skim that chapter to locate the specific verse.

If you want to read online, enter the reference into BibleGateway.com or BibleHub.com. Also check out the YouVersion app.

Learn more about the greatest book ever written at ABibleADay.com, which provides a Bible blog, summaries of the books of the Bible, a dictionary of Bible terms, Bible reading plans, and other resources.

ABOUT PETER DEHAAN

Peter DeHaan, PhD, wants to change the world one word at a time. His books and blog posts discuss God, the Bible, and church, geared toward spiritual seekers and church dropouts. Many people feel church has let them down, and Peter seeks to encourage them as they search for a place to belong.

But he's not afraid to ask tough questions or make religious people squirm. He's not trying to be provocative. Instead, he seeks truth, even if it makes people uncomfortable. Peter urges Christians to push past the status quo and reexamine how they practice their faith in every part of their lives.

Peter earned his doctorate, awarded with high distinction, from Trinity College of the Bible and Theological Seminary. He lives with his wife in beautiful Southwest Michigan and wrangles cross-word puzzles in his spare time.

A lifelong student of Scripture, Peter wrote the 1,000-page website ABibleADay.com to encourage people to explore the Bible, the greatest book ever written. His popular blog, at PeterDeHaan.com, addresses biblical Christianity to build a faith that matters.

Read his blog, receive his newsletter, and learn more at PeterDeHaan.com.

BOOKS BY PETER DEHAAN

40-Day Bible Study Series

Dear Theophilus (the Gospel of Luke)

Acts Bible Study

Isaiah Bible Study

Dear Theophilus, Minor Prophets

Dear Theophilus, Job

Living Water (John)

Love Is Patient (1 and 2 Corinthians)

Revelation Bible Study

Love One Another (1, 2, and 3 John)

Run with Perseverance (Hebrews)

James and Jude Bible Study

Matthew Bible Study

1 & 2 Peter Bible Study

Mark Bible Study

Holiday Celebration Devotionals

The Advent of Jesus

The Passion of Jesus (a Lenten devotional)

The Victory of Jesus (an Easter devotional)

The Ministry of Jesus

Thanksgiving with Jesus

Bible Character Sketches Series

Women of the Bible

The Friends and Foes of Jesus

Old Testament Sinners and Saints

More Old Testament Sinners and Saints

Heroes and Heavies of the Apocrypha

200 Old Testament Sinners and Saints

Visiting Churches Series

52 Churches

The 52 Churches Workbook

More Than 52 Churches

The More Than 52 Churches Workbook

Visiting Online Church

Shopping for Church

Other Books

Elephant God

Jesus's Broken Church

Martin Luther's 95 Theses

The Christian Church's LGBTQ Failure

Bridging the Sacred-Secular Divide

Beyond Psalm 150

How Big Is Your Tent?

For the latest list of all Peter's books, go to
PeterDeHaan.com/books.

www.ingramcontent.com/pod-product-compliance
Lightning Source LLC
Chambersburg PA
CBHW071747120626
46550CB00002B/702